124ρ

Psychotherapy of
Neurotic Character

Also by David Shapiro

Neurotic Styles
Autonomy and Rigid Character

PSYCHOTHERAPY

OF NEUROTIC

CHARACTER

DAVID SHAPIRO

Basic Books, Inc., Publishers

NEW YORK

Library of Congress Cataloging-in-Publication Data

Shapiro, David, 1926–
  Psychotherapy of neurotic character.

  Includes bibliographical references and index.
  1. Neuroses—Treatment. 2. Psychotherapy.
WM 170 S529p]
RC530.S52 1989   616.85'2   88–47894
ISBN 0–465–06750–6

To the memory of my father, Jack,
and my mother, Ella

CONTENTS

PREFACE

My teacher, Hellmuth Kaiser, once expressed a dilemma to me about the teaching of psychotherapy. He said it was no use teaching what to do or what to say because the significance and effect of what the therapist did or said depended on the attitude with which it was expressed. With the right attitude on the part of the therapist, he thought, all else would follow easily. I am not sure that in fact all else does follow easily, but in any case, how does one teach an attitude? For example, how does one teach an attitude of respect for the patient, not merely courtesy and not sentimental concern, but respect for the patient's psychology? How, for that matter, can one teach an interest in the patient, not merely an interest in changing him, but an interest in him and in communicating with him? I think these attitudes and interests can be developed—taught in a sense—but certainly not directly, not merely by recommending them. They can be developed only through a certain kind of understanding of the patient. Understanding can engender a therapeutic attitude.

My earlier work has sometimes been described as "phenomenological." In our field, this term usually means relying on or even limiting oneself to the immediate data of subjective experience. It is true that I have been interested in studying the formal ways of thinking, the attitudes, the kinds of subjective experience, and the kinds of behavior that characterize various types of neurotic conditions. But my interest has never been purely descriptive. Rather, I have been interested in studying the ways in which neurotic personalities work, particularly in showing that specific kinds of symptoms are products or special instances of such neurotic styles—that they are products, in other words, of characteristic mentalities. For example, it is possible to show that the paranoid defense mechanism of projection is not an elementary device but a special result of the workings of a certain kind of rigid personality, a personality of certain attitudes and ways of thinking, under particular conditions of subjective tension. Similarly, such symptoms as compulsive rituals or strange, often discomforting, obsessive thoughts can be shown to be not the intrusions into normal rational life that they may seem but special products of a kind of scrupulousness that, though not consciously articulated, characterizes the subjective life of certain individuals. In short, if one studies not only the symptom but also the subjective life and the mentality of the *person* in whom it appears, symptoms or symptomatic reactions that seem and feel like irrational intrusions into everyday rational thought and attitude actually make some kind of subjective sense.

The question arises, What distinguishes *neurotic* styles or character from nonneurotic ways or dispositions of the personality? The answer was not at all clear to me at first, though, once recognized, it hardly seems subtle. The neurotic personality or character—I will use the terms interchangeably—is one that reacts against itself; it reacts, reflexively, against certain of its own tendencies. It is a personality in conflict. Thus a picture of neurotic *dynamics* emerges from a study of neurotic *styles*. But it is a picture of dynamics of a rather unaccustomed kind, different from the more familiar dynamics of impulse and defense.

The dynamics of neurotic styles is the dynamics, the workings, of the *personality*. It includes not merely conflict between particular wish and defense but the reaction of general restrictive attitudes to whole classes of subjective experience. It is a dynamics of the neurotic person as distinct from a dynamics of a nuclear neurotic conflict that affects the person.

In this picture of the dynamics of the person, subjective experience is not merely a reflection or a result of essential dynamic processes, as it is sometimes considered; rather, it is central to those dynamics. Subjective sensation and fleeting idea, momentary direction of interest and attention, the particular quality of a discomfort, may all be largely unrecognized and unarticulated yet play a central role in triggering inhibitory reactions of the personality. Thus the dynamics of the personality is also a dynamics of subjective experience. It involves reactions and processes (as I will try to show) that are neither clearly articulated in consciousness nor, strictly speaking, unconscious.

This view of neurotic personality or character gives substantial meaning to the precept that the neurotic problem is not *in* the patient, it *is* the patient, and to its corollary, that the patient himself, not only what the patient provides, is the therapeutic material. These principles, which doubtless would be acceptable as such to most therapists, have more far-reaching implications for the conduct of psychotherapy and the understanding of patients than might be imagined, if they are understood in this way and applied consistently. They affect the nature of the therapist's interest in the patient and turn his attention to the patient in a somewhat different way. They extend the therapist's interest beyond the usual textual scrutiny of what the patient says to include the patient's whole subjective world. It is when the therapist introduces the patient to this world—to the subjective experience that the patient lives but does not know he lives—that a therapeutic effect is achieved.

The book is divided into three parts, the first of which is "Neurotic Character and Psychotherapy: General Principles." In chapter 1, I will indicate briefly the relation I mean to develop between neurotic personality and psychotherapy, focusing especially on the neurotic person's estrangement from himself, while in the next chapter, I will elaborate the conception of neurotic personality. Part two, "The Therapeutic Material," is composed of three chapters. Two of these chapters explain and apply the conception of the therapeutic material to which I have already referred; the third considers the therapeutic relationship as therapeutic material. Part three, "The Therapeutic Process," includes a chapter on the psychology of therapeutic change followed by one on the significance of the therapeutic relationship for such change. I have introduced then a chapter on the important question of historical interpretation in psychotherapy. The book's last chapter considers certain aspects of the course of therapy in more detail.

I wish to add a note here about the clinical examples I have used throughout the book. I have, of course, disguised the identity of these patients—some of them patients of others whose treatment I have supervised—by changing or omitting all identifying details of description. I do not believe that these alterations have significantly affected the instructive value (as distinct from scientific value) of the examples. I use these clinical examples to illustrate and clarify psychological processes that are comparatively fundamental in nature and therefore very common, not only among patients in psychotherapy but among all human beings. These purposes do not require any significant amount of biographical material, and the symptomatology involved is far from unique.

ACKNOWLEDGMENTS

I particularly wish to express my gratitude to my friends Dr. Jean G. Schimek of New York University and Alford, Massachusetts, and Dr. Deborah L. Browning of Lakeville, Connecticut, for their help in the preparation of this book. Their close critical reading of the entire manuscript—in Dr. Schimek's case, discussion of many parts of it with me more than once—has been enormously valuable. Of like importance has been the help of my wife, Gerry Shapiro, and I should like to express my appreciation to her. My friend Dr. David Gordon of Los Angeles also helped me clarify certain portions of the manuscript concerned with the philosophy of language.

PART ONE

Neurotic Character and Psychotherapy: General Principles

All names, identifying characteristics,
and other details of the case material
in this book have been changed.

Chapter 1

Neurotic Self-Estrangement and Psychotherapy

Self-Estrangement

In neurosis the personality reacts against itself. It seems that the person has tendencies that his own character cannot tolerate and reacts against, with remarkable consequences. We shall consider this reaction later in some detail. Here I want to note only one consequence of it—the most remarkable one—the discovery, or, at least, the scientific understanding, of which was probably Freud's most fundamental achievement. I am referring to the fact that such a reaction by the personality against itself leaves the person who experiences it estranged, cut off, from himself in certain ways. He does not know what he wants or what he wants to do. He does not know what he feels; or sometimes he knows he has strong feelings or reactions but they seem strange to him, as in the case of phobias, mysteriously at odds with his judgment, attitudes, or common sense.

Such self-estrangement is perhaps the most definitive feature of neurotic personality and also of neurotic symptoms. It is true that mere eccentricity of behavior or reaction, like the oddness of some compulsive rituals, can itself suggest internal neurotic processes, but it is not an absolutely reliable indicator. After all, odd behavior may signify nothing more than an unfamiliar purpose—say, a religious purpose—from which standpoint that behavior, odd to the ignorant observer, makes perfectly clear sense. By contrast, the neurotic process results in the subject's loss of a sense of the purpose of, or connection with, his own behavior, as in a feeling of not having intended or wished to do what one has done or is doing, or a sense of estrangement from his own feeling, impulse, or reaction. This kind of experience is present in neurosis (and in psychosis) in a great variety of subjective forms. Some of them are subjectively conspicuous, such as the experience of being compelled, even against one's will, to carry out some ritual, or the experience of being swept by an "irresistible impulse." Other forms of the experience of self-estrangement are hardly noticed subjectively, especially if they are more or less continuous and long familiar. Thus there is the feeling, regular among some people, of not having wanted or "meant" to do something but being forced by circumstances or tempted beyond one's power to resist; or the feeling of living one's whole life not as one wanted but as required by obligations or as dictated by others' expectations; or simply the feeling of having no idea what one wants to do.

Here is an example of symptomatic self-estrangement: A very intelligent, ambitious, young businesswoman has had a very troubled and highly emotional relationship with the man she has been living with. It is easy to tell from her description that each day she returns home eagerly. Yet she is hardly in the house before an argument erupts, started usually by her dissatisfaction with some behavior of his.

She begins her therapy hour in an agitated way: "What's the *matter* with me? I've got to end this thing! There's nothing in it for me! I get nothing out of it! I can't even talk to him! He has nothing to say! He's a nothing! I get nothing out of it, yet I can't seem to end it! Why do I continue it? It's like an addiction! . . ."

This woman says, "I get nothing out of it," but we know that cannot be true. We would know this even if we did not know how eagerly she returns home each evening. Yet when she says, "I get nothing out of it," she is quite sincere. The feelings of affection for her companion that have been evident to the therapist and are reflected in her eagerness to return home every day are reduced in her awareness to the quality of an "addiction." How can we explain this phenomenon?

The way she talks about him and, even more, about herself ("What's the *matter* with me?") provides a clue. She talks angrily and reproachfully, chiding and berating herself for continuing this relationship. She is not so much speaking to the therapist as remonstrating with herself, underscoring her point with exaggerated evidence ("He's a nothing!"). Each statement she makes is an imperative, directed at herself and requiring only a change in pronoun to reproduce a parent's reproachful warning to a wayward child ("What's the *matter* with [you]?"). She disapproves less of him than of herself. (To be exact, she does not simply disapprove of what she is doing—if she did, she would stop—but of not wanting to stop, of wanting to continue doing it.) That disapproval is conspicuous to someone else, yet it is largely invisible to the patient herself. It is experienced by her, but it is not visible to her. In her view, she is merely frustrated by her "addiction" to a relationship that offers her nothing, frustrated by her inexplicable weakness. In her view, if she disapproves of anything, it is only of this "addiction." In our view, it is just the other way around: the intensity of her disapproval narrows her awareness of her own feelings to the point that she can identify them only as an addiction.

The therapy hour continues:

> PATIENT: I can't seem to end it! *Why* do I continue it? It's like an addiction!
>
> THERAPIST *(suggesting a perfectly evident, psychologically more comprehensible—if, to the patient, unwelcome— possibility):* Perhaps you're in love with him.
>
> PATIENT *(looking somewhat flustered, but indignant):* That's impossible!
>
> THERAPIST: "That's impossible" does not sound quite the same as "I'm not."

Finally, still grudgingly, she talks about him. She sounds then quite different: she sounds more conversational whereas before she had sounded as if she were making a speech. She even begins to talk about him quite affectionately, though still uncomfortably. He is good-looking, amusing, a nice fellow; but he is not at all the sort of man she had in mind for herself, not, she says, the sort who was "right" or "appropriate" for her.

It is not remarkable that someone should disapprove of a wish or an interest of theirs and feel conflict for that reason; nor is such conflict on that account neurotic. Rather, the remarkable thing is that an unarticulated and reflexive reaction against one's own feelings should have the effect of narrowing the awareness of those feelings to the sensation of a quasi-alien "addiction." The remarkable thing, in other words, is that this woman's reaction to her affection for this "inappropriate" man should obliterate awareness of her wish to be with him. Thus each day this patient leaves work eagerly for home, without recognizing her own eagerness. As she draws closer to home, she begins, without noticing it, to remonstrate with herself much as she did in the therapy hour; and shortly after her arrival, feeling angry with him for being "inappropriate," she picks a fight. She "can't seem to" leave him because, though she does not realize it, she does not want to. But she cannot stay with him comfortably either.

As I said, it is neither remarkable nor neurotic that people experience internal conflict. The world of possibilities and the nature of anyone's interests in those possibilities are not, after all, simple matters. But this conflict is of a special and more complicated kind. It is not a conflict among clear external possibilities. It contains a reaction against the self that distorts awareness of one's interests in those possibilities. Hence the intrinsic nature of this conflict stands in the way of its resolution. At least, its peculiar nature disqualifies the efforts of its subject to resolve it, unaided.

The following example is in some ways comparable. A rather exaggeratedly "manly" man describes, somewhat defensively, his wife's complaint about him—that he never talks to her. Apparently he responds to her complaint with an abrupt "All right, what do you want to talk about?" and she walks away, hurt. But after he describes this scene to the therapist, he says, somewhat grudgingly, that he realizes what she actually wants. She wants him to tell her that he loves her, as she has often made plain. But, he adds, he simply "cannot" do that—"I don't know why, but I can't." It is not clear, however, whether he says that he cannot do that regretfully or stubbornly.

THERAPIST: Do you mean, then, that if you could, you would like to?

PATIENT: Well, I don't know. . . . Maybe I can't say it because I'm not sure it's true. Maybe I don't love her.

THERAPIST: Certainly it's possible that you don't, but you do seem to be quite careful in what you say to her not to go too far.

The patient seems to consider, then says, carefully, that "probably" he does love her; even so, he adds, he can't tell her that he does.

The therapist observes that he seems hardly to be able to say it here, let alone to her; that he says he "probably" loves her as if he were admitting something.

At this, the patient becomes silent. Then he says a striking thing. He recalls that as a young man, he told other women that he loved them when he knew perfectly well that he did not. It was the thing to say; they expected it; so he said it. But with his wife—and here his voice becomes a little unsteady—it would feel "mushy" and "soft," sentimental.

It turns out, in other words, that he cannot say such a thing to his wife precisely because he *would* mean it, and feel it, which would be abhorrent to him. It feels soft and unmanly.

Here again the person is in conflict with himself, and he is cut off from the nature of that conflict and from the subjective world that gives rise to it by the conflict itself. His initially unarticulated anxiety about going "soft" prompts him, in a quasi-reflexive way, to act more "manly" and thus to reassure himself. The reassuring result of that reaction protects him from recognizing the nature of the anxiety that prompted it.

In ordinary human intercourse, we are accustomed to a different sort of situation. We expect others to explain their points of view, to tell us, or at least to be able to tell us, what they have in mind, how this or that behavior or reaction makes sense, or why it is reasonable, when we do not understand it or feel particularly sympathetic to it. The woman who jostles us in getting to her seat on the bus explains that she has been on her feet all day and we are placated. Even if she does not take the trouble to explain, it can ordinarily be assumed that she for one understands her situation and is sympathetic to it, even if we are not. Yet in the examples I have cited, something of the reverse seems to be the case.

The neurotic person is estranged from his own reasons because those reasons are themselves the subject of conflict. He is estranged from his own reasons by reactions and prejudices of which he is also unaware; often he is not even sympathetically disposed to understand that he has his reasons. We, however, are outside his conflict and his particular prejudices, and this is our great advantage in helping him. Our knowledge does not qualify us to help ourselves in comparable circumstances, but we are in a position to help him. We can be interested in him without prejudice, in particular without the disqualifying and consciousness-distorting reaction he has to himself. We are able to assume he *has* his reasons even when he is not able to make that assumption. We become aware that the young woman is not so much talking to us as remonstrating with herself, when she cannot be aware of it, precisely because at that moment she is bent on remonstrance, not on understanding. We can notice, as she cannot, that for all its intensity, her disapproval is not wholehearted, that there is even the suggestion of affection, perhaps more than affection, in her voice. We can recognize that the man who says he might love his wife says so as if he were admitting something, when he cannot possibly recognize that, precisely because to him it is something to admit. Thus we are in a position to help these people. We cannot read their minds, but we are free from their disqualifications. We are in a position to introduce them to themselves. We can restore their awareness of their own wishes and feelings, and their awareness, as well, of their reactions against those wishes and feelings. In this way we hope to be able to transform an intrinsically unresolvable neurotic conflict, a reflexive and inaccessible reaction against the self, into an ordinary conflict of possibilities.

I have chosen my examples for the comparative transparency of their immediate conflict and of the immediate basis of their self-estrangement; but this transparency is not typical of neurotic symptoms. Nevertheless all symptoms—not just the classical ones such as obsessions, compulsions, and such, but all symptomatic behavior or reaction in the broadest sense—have this general form: they are products of conflict from which their subject is largely cut off. This self-estrangement is not always obvious, certainly not to the subject himself, who may rationalize his symptoms in various ways, or may simply be accustomed to them. But it is always true. Indeed, it is a truism, for it is, more than anything else, the definition of symptomatic behavior or reaction.

Psychotherapy

It is our idea in psychotherapy to introduce the neurotic person to himself, but not merely in the sense of informing him about himself, about the existence of his inner conflict or even about its nature or history. That would probably not help him much more than telling him his diagnosis. Our aim is actually to enlarge his experience of himself, specifically to enlarge his experience of, and to make possible the articulation of, the feelings and thoughts involved in that conflict, and in this way to create the conditions for its resolution.

This process involves, in my opinion, the recognition by the therapist—or, sometimes, the articulation by him—of feelings or attitudes of the patient that are in a certain sense already conscious and actually already within subjective experience, yet are not—and for certain reasons that we shall presently consider cannot be—fully articulated or recognized by the patient himself. In proposing this—I shall give an example in a moment—I am calling attention to a kind of self-estrangement and to a level of subjective experience and mental activity that, though I believe they are perfectly well known to all of us, are not usually identified in the literature of psychotherapy[1] and are not unambiguously identified in the traditional psychoanalytic division of mental processes into conscious, preconscious, and unconscious.[2] It is the articulation of this kind of unar-

[1]Carl Rogers's psychotherapy does seem to focus on this level of subjective experience—at least certain aspects of it—though he does not make this completely explicit. Neither does he seem to distinguish clearly between subjective experience that cannot be articulated spontaneously by the patient and that which can.

[2]Although, of course, the existence of levels and varieties of conscious experience is well recognized in psychoanalytic literature. See, for example, David Rapaport's (1951) discussion of the "infinitely multitudinous . . . varieties of conscious experience" and especially his distinction between awareness and "reflective awareness": "States of Consciousness: A Psychopathological and Psychodynamic View," in *The Collected Papers of David Rapaport,* Merton M. Gill, ed. (New York: Basic Books, 1967), pp. 385–404. The psychoanalytic term "preconscious" would be convenient here and would immediately establish a consistency with psychoanalytic technique, but it is unfortunately not quite suitable. "Preconscious" usually refers to that which is outside of conscious awareness, but only for lack of attention, not for dynamic reasons. The subjective experience to which I am referring, by contrast, *cannot* be consciously articulated spontaneously *for* dynamic reasons. It is true, however, that "preconscious" is somewhat ambiguous in this respect, and Freud did speak of a "second censorship" between consciousness and the preconscious (see Sigmund Freud, "The Unconscious" [1915], *Standard Edition,* 14:193 [London: Hogarth Press, 1957]). The psycho-

ticulated, unrecognized, or unreflective subjective experience that can produce an immediate therapeutic effect.

In the following example, as it happens, the patient does inattentively articulate a certain feeling and thought, yet he remains unable to recognize their existence spontaneously. Although he has not been asked to do so, this young man explains his difficult decision to take a certain job. He concludes with an exaggerated and forceful assertion of confidence:

> PATIENT: I'm *sure* it's the right thing to do! . . . I guess.
> THERAPIST: You *guess.*

The mere underscoring of the patient's word, which he had originally added with his voice trailing off and without seeming to notice its significance, produces an immediate effect. He seems surprised and flustered; he starts to object; then he laughs. He proceeds to describe his doubts—can he get along with the boss? might a better job come along? and so forth— still reluctantly—he is afraid, it turns out, that he will "succumb" to doubting and neurotic weakness—but talking now in a quieter and more genuine way.

This man's initial subjective experience cannot have been self-confidence. He thought he felt self-confident, he asserted his self-confidence, he tried to act—one might say he tried to

---

therapeutic work presented here could be described as work on that "second censorship," if one wishes to put it in such terms; indeed, it could be argued from a strictly psychoanalytic standpoint that work on that level is the only possibility for effective therapeutic interpretation. Otto Fenichel says, *"To begin with, we only work against this second censorship"* (italics in original; see "Concerning the Theory of Psychoanalytic Technique," in *The Collected Papers of Otto Fenichel, First Series,* ed. Hanna Fenichel and David Rapaport [New York: W. W. Norton, 1953]). But it is difficult to see why, if that is good practice to begin with, it should be abandoned later, inasmuch as the second censorship must be presumed to continue to exist.

feel—self-confident. But the look in his eyes, the quality of his voice, perhaps above all the exaggerated assertion of self-assuredness itself, were the expressions of one who feels self-doubt. It may be assumed, in fact, that the dim sensation of that very doubt was what prompted his efforts—unrecognized and unarticulated, of course, as any process of self-deception must be—to persuade himself and the therapist of his confidence in his decision.

That process of denial produces a distortion of his awareness of himself, an estrangement from the actual quality of his own subjective experience and thought, from his actual frame of mind. It is worth noting that this process also has the effect of estranging him from the quality of his objective circumstances. The therapist's articulation, in this instance merely emphasizing the patient's unnoticed allusion to that subjective experience, immediately brings the patient into contact with it: in other words, it brings him into contact with himself. For the time being at least, he abandons his efforts to deny to himself the various doubts and concerns that surely have passed fleetingly and unrecognized through his awareness even while he denies them, and he is able, therefore, to express and consider them. In this form, the conflict is susceptible to resolution in a way that it was not before. As long as his doubts are denied conscious articulation he is driven, both by them and by the equally unarticulated necessity to deny them, in contradictory directions. As soon as they become articulated, both concerns become matters of consideration. This shift from an artificial self-confidence at odds with actual subjective experience to a more genuine and integrated state exemplifies the nature of therapeutic change.

Chapter 2

Neurotic Character

A method of psychotherapy is naturally dependent on a conception of neurotic problems. It is not possible, however, to proceed with a discussion of psychotherapy while taking for granted the existence of any such clear, coherent, and commonly accepted conception. It does not exist. The only widely accepted, logically coherent theory of neurosis today remains the classical conflict theory of psychoanalysis. It has shown itself to have great explanatory power. But that theory can now be seen to have serious inadequacies; in fact, in certain respects it has been superseded by developments in psychoanalysis itself. The study of psychopathology is not a field, like physics, of clearly defined principles, logical cohesiveness, universally recognized data, and critical experiments. In such a field, disagreement is sharp and within a reasonable time comes to a decisive conclusion. But our field is loose, not logically cohesive; a conclusion in one area is not easily applied to another; what seems to be a theoretical advance appears to have no application to practice at all. Accordingly, old ideas, no longer tenable, continue to have currency and are even taught side by side with newer ones with which they are not logically compatible; discarded notions continually reappear; and, in general, our field is full of its own history.

In this chapter I shall discuss the nature of neurotic conditions in more detail. Specifically, I will present a *characterological* understanding of neurosis. I mean by this term that neurosis consists not of a nuclear conflict within the person—such as between particular unconscious impulse and defense—but of a distortion of the whole personality. Neurosis consists of certain restrictive and conflict-generating ways in which the personality works, certain ways in which, as I put it earlier, the personality reacts against itself. I have used the term "neurotic style" in the same sense.[1] From this standpoint, the old distinction between "symptom neurosis" and "character disorder" disappears; all neurosis is characterological.

History and Problems

In order to bring this idea of neurosis into sharper focus, I shall refer to some historical matters—to Freud's earliest, pre-psychoanalytic conception of neurosis and to the development of the classical psychoanalytic conflict theory. Some aspects of this theoretical development point to such a characterological understanding.

It should be remembered that Freud's earliest understanding of neurosis, initially in collaboration with Breuer, at the end of the nineteenth century, had very little to do with personal-

[1]David Shapiro, *Neurotic Styles* (New York: Basic Books, 1965).

ity. It was a theory of the specific source of the specific symptom, such as a hysterical paralysis, a tic, or a specific inhibition. Freud took some pains, in fact, to stress the essential normality (except for the symptom), as well as the respectability, of his early patients. He clearly wished to distinguish his view from those psychiatric views of the time—actually in a sense more characterological views—that regarded neurosis as a sign of a biologically or morally (as in malingering) defective person. As is well known, Freud's earliest theory was of accidental, diverse trauma, which he later developed into a theory of sexual trauma and seduction by the father. The trauma and therefore the neurosis were accidental in the sense that they involved external circumstances that had no relation to the victim's personality. There was perhaps only the suggestion that the patients' very refinement had rendered them more sensitive.

According to the trauma theory, the symptom was the symbolic manifestation of dammed-up affect, a kind of toxic condition. It was the product of an event that was originally unassimilable and was therefore dissociated from the personality, to be revived—according to the sexual seduction theory—at puberty and to erupt symbolically into a symptom sometime thereafter. Thus both neurosis and symptom were essentially isolated from the personality. It is only reasonable that they should have been, considering the nature of the problem that Freud was trying to solve. Above all, that problem was to explain the strangeness of the symptom, which was mysterious precisely because it was, to all appearances, utterly unrelated to the conscious mind and to an otherwise unremarkable personality. Freud was seeking the cause of an illness, an *intrusion into the personality*. The illness was found in the abcesslike dissociated memory; the cause was the trauma. The therapy was catharsis or abreaction, the draining of the abcess. The

16

nature of the therapy was determined by the nature of the condition, perhaps more unequivocally than it was to be ever again.

We know that before long Freud became dissatisfied with this theory. He said, and it is usually accepted, that he lost confidence in the proposition that all neurotic patients could actually have had experiences of seduction.[2] Whatever its promptings, his new, alternative theory—namely that the repressed sexual memories were not of actual experiences but of fantasies—was psychologically much more profound and far-reaching. For in the new theory the neurosis was no longer a result of an external, passively experienced accident; it was now seen as an intrinsic product, not exactly of the personality, but certainly of the person. The abandonment of the trauma theory in favor of the the fantasy theory signals the beginning of the developmental theory of the libido, the psychosexual development believed to give rise to the fantasy. At the same time, it presents us with the classical form of the internal conflict theory of neurosis: the source of the neurosis is the childhood conflict between the drive and the defense against it.

It does not seem too much to say that each step Freud's thinking took in this evolution—from a theory of diverse trauma, to sexual trauma, to sexual trauma at the hands of the father, to childhood sexual fantasy—conceives of a deeper and more intrinsic rooting of the neurosis in the individual's psychology and reflects, further, an increasing interest in a general human psychology. At the same time, that conceptual evolution corresponds to the therapeutic transition from the use of

[2]Jean G. Schimek has pointed out that Freud's evidence of the original pathogenic sexual seduction never actually included unambiguous recovery of memories of it, but relied heavily on what Freud construed as a "reproduction" of the event in the therapy situation: see "Fact and Fantasy in the Seduction Theory: An Historical Review," *Journal of the American Psychoanalytical Association* 35, no. 4 (1987): 937–65.

hypnosis, directly aimed at the recovery and abreaction of the trauma, to a directed association technique, and finally to the psychoanalytic method of free-ranging association, with its interest in finding derivatives of the infantile conflict in whatever associative connection they might turn up. As is well known, the psychoanalytic interest at that time was in the discovery of the fantasies and impulses that lay beneath consciousness and in their expression not only in symptoms but also—in symbolic, derivative ways—in nonpathological products of the mind: in dreams, artistic productions, wit, slips of the tongue, and so forth. The impressive discoveries of the time, both in psychopathology and in these other areas, were of such expressions from below.

As important as this development was, certain essential features of the original trauma conception of neurosis were naturally retained. The neurosis was no longer externally caused or accidental and was now seen as derived from sources intrinsic to the person; yet still it initially remained, in conception, largely isolated from the personality—and with good reason. The isolation or dissociation of the neurotic conflict from rational adult consciousness—from the adult personality and attitudes—remained, after all, essential to its value in explaining symptoms that were themselves (or seemed to be) alien to the adult personality. Thus the infantile neurotic conflict constituted a nuclear pathological agent causing the patient to behave—as in the case, say, of compulsive rituals—according to "aims" of *its* dynamics; that is, according to some derivative of his unconscious infantile aims. Sometimes these unconscious aims, deriving from the infantile conflict, might be rationalized and sometimes not; but in any case they remained distinct from the person's conscious aims. The neurotic symptom, a manifestation of the unconscious conflict in the form of some compromise between the repressed wish and the repressing forces, remained *an irrational intrusion* into the adult attitudes of consciousness.

It is possible now to see that a paradox was raised by this conception and these discoveries. On the one hand, this classical picture of neurosis established the neurotic symptom as a medical-psychological problem, not only in its being scientifically understandable but also in the sense of being beyond the patient's volitional control. Yet on the other, this conception works a certain distortion on the picture of living people. In its one-sided emphasis on the striving of unconscious drives or wishes toward the satisfaction of "their" aims, there was danger of creating a picture of the living person, as Erik Erikson put it, as a kind of marionette.[3] And this distortion is especially apparent in the picture of the neurotic person and of unconsciously motivated symptomatic reactions or behavior. The conception of an unconscious agent of behavior, an anomalous and irrational intruder into adult attitudes, rescued neurosis for scientific understanding and the possibility of treatment. But at the same time, and apparently unavoidably, it clouded the individual's responsibility for his own behavior, seeming to make him a mere passive—or even unwilling—witness of it. In general, this concept unrealistically reduced the role of the individual's consciousness to that of a compliant and innocuous bystander.[4]

The one-sided interest in the repressed had another, more immediate deficiency as far as clinical understanding was concerned. That deficiency, which came to be well-recognized,

---

[3]Erik H. Erikson, *Childhood and Society* (New York: W. W. Norton, 1950). p. 60.

[4]For a more extensive discussion of this problem, see David Shapiro, *Autonomy and Rigid Character* (New York: Basic Books, 1981).

was the problem of the so-called "choice of neurosis," the determination of the specific nature of neurotic symptoms and behavior. Indeed, this problem was bound to remain intractable as long as the neurosis was conceived as a nuclear conflict, preserved from childhood and more or less separated from the adult personality and the attitudes and ways of consciousness. Perhaps the best example of the problem is the most famous one, Freud's discovery of a relation between unconscious homosexuality and paranoia.[5] It has been described justifiably as one of the most striking and incontrovertible discoveries in psychiatry. But it was, also, conspicuously limited, one-sided, in its understanding of that relation—a limitation, incidentally, that Freud recognized clearly at the time. The striking element in Freud's discovery was the evidence, in the *Memoirs* of the paranoid jurist Schreber (and later amply confirmed in innumerable cases of male paranoia), of an intense, though consciously unrecognized and abhorrent, homosexual interest underlying Schreber's dreadful delusions of being "unmanned" and transformed by God into a wanton and sensuous female.[6] It was clearly the intensity of Schreber's abhorrence of this sexual wish that required its disavowal. And that disavowal was accomplished by the paranoid, or projective, defense through which the intolerable internal conflict was transformed into a struggle against an external threat. But why this particular defense? Why not, say, simple repression? The theory does not provide an explanation. For that matter, the theory does not explain, as Robert P. Knight has pointed out, why this person developed in the first place "such an intense homosexual wish-

[5]Sigmund Freud, "Psychoanalytic Notes on an Autobiographical Account of a Case of Paranoia" (1911), *Standard Edition*, 12:9–82 (London: Hogarth Press, 1958).
[6]Daniel P. Schreber, *Memoirs of My Mental Illness*, trans. Ida MacAlpine and Richard A. Hunter (London: William Dawson, 1955).

fantasy nor why he must deny it so desperately."[7] These gaps in Freud's theory are traceable not to any failure to recognize the underlying wish but to the absence of a picture of the personality, the ways of thinking, and the attitudes of the person in whom it appears.

The problem of the "choice of neurosis" is by no means a problem of theoretical interest alone. If one is in the dark about the determinants—I am speaking about the personality determinants, not the historical ones—of the specific form of symptomatic behavior or reaction, then one is in the dark about a great deal that might be of value to the therapist. These determinants, for example, include the specific subjective experience of, say, the anxiety about and abhorrence of homosexual wishes that prompts one particular reaction and no other. In other words, if one is in the dark about the "choice of neurosis" in this sense, one is in the dark about the specific subjective psychology of the neurotic conflict.

Thus, formulations of neurotic conflict that are limited to drive and defense—such as the formulation that paranoia is a defense against unconscious homosexuality—suffer from three limitations at the same stroke. First, the neurotic person, especially in the instance of symptomatic behavior, tends to be depicted as if he were a marionette operated by those forces. Second, in such a formulation there is no indication of the determinants of the specific symptomatology. Finally, there is no indication of the individual form and quality of the subjective experience that accounts for the specific reactions and behaviors. These three limitations are essentially one: classical dynamic formulations of nuclear neurotic conflicts do not include the processes and reactions of subjective experience,

[7]Robert P. Knight, "The Relationship of Latent Homosexuality to the Mechanism of Paranoid Delusions," *Bulletin of the Menninger Clinic* 4 (1940): 149–59.

those largely unarticulated attitudes of consciousness and workings of the mind that make up one's experience of oneself and that determine specifically individual behavior and personal reaction.

Freud's interest and that of psychoanalysis shifted from interest only in what was repressed to interest in the agencies of repression as well. This shift is represented, theoretically, in the development and elaboration of the concept of the ego. As far as the conceptions of neurosis and psychotherapy are concerned, that development, I believe, had its most significant expression and greatest influence in the characterological work of Wilhelm Reich.[8] It was this work (to which I shall return later), perhaps more than any other, that implemented the shift in therapeutic emphasis from interpetation of the repressed infantile wish to interpretation of the defense against that wish. It went further: it explicitly enlarged the conception of neurosis beyond the original nuclear conflict of childhood wish and defense to include distortions of the entire personality or character. Reich's proposal that the principal neurotic defense, and therefore the principal resistance in the analysis, consisted of the patient's character itself, his "ways of being," the "formal aspects of his general behavior," clearly called for a redirection of the therapist's attention from the search for derivatives or manifestations of the repressed wish to the attitudes of the restrictive neurotic personality. In fact, his conception came very close to abandoning the classical conception of the nuclear drive-defense conflict altogether. It is true that he conceived of these restrictive "ways of being" as having originated entirely in the circumstances of the infantile nuclear conflict, a position general psychological evidence could never support (and a position that later psychoanalysis, with its recog-

[8]Wilhelm Reich, *Character Analysis* (New York: Orgone Institute Press, 1949).

nition of independent "conflict-free" contributions to the ego, would no longer require). But Reich's conception made it clear that these "ways" were, in adults, generalized and "hardened" into "chronic automatic modes of reaction." While Reich does not say so, his conceptions often suggest that the neurotic problem is not in the person or acting on the person; rather it *is* the person. To have taken that step and substantiated it would have been to dissolve the "marionette" problem in a stroke.

Since then, various developments in and around the theoretical mainstream of psychoanalysis have considerably mitigated the early "marionette" conception. The conscious person, particularly in his adaptive capacity, has received more adequate recognition by psychoanalytic ego psychology than by earlier psychoanalytic theory. Erikson, a notable example, significantly broadened the traditional conceptions of psychosexual development and conflict and their possible outcomes to include general attitudes (such as trust or mistrust) and modes of behavior.[9] He thereby transformed that conception from one of the development of *drives* to one of the development of *children*. More recent psychoanalytic criticism of traditional "metapsychological" concepts such as drive and drive energy, in favor of concepts closer to subjective experience,[10] is consistent with this trend, as is, to some extent, the contribution of the psychoanalytic school of "self-psychology."[11]

[9]Erikson, *Childhood and Society* [3].

[10]See, for example, Robert R. Holt, "Drive or Wish: A Reconsideration of the Psychoanalytic Theory of Motivation," *Psychological Issues* 9, no. 4, monograph 36 (n.d.): 158–97; and George S. Klein, *Psychoanalytic Theory: An Exploration of Essentials* (New York: International Universities Press, 1976); also Roy Schafer, *A New Language for Psychoanalysis* (New Haven: Yale University Press, 1976).

[11]See Heinz Kohut, *The Analysis of the Self* (New York: International Universities Press, 1971) and his *The Restoration of the Self* (New York: International Universities Press, 1977).

In the course of this development, the psychiatric picture of neurosis and of neurotic symptoms has changed. Many observers, indeed, have maintained that neurotic conditions and their symptoms themselves have changed since Freud's day; but if that is so, there is no doubt that the psychiatric conception of them has changed as well. The completely ego-alien symptom, seemingly isolated from the personality, is nowadays in doubt or considered a rarity. Symptoms are recognized as more characterological in the sense of being typically fairly general features of attitude, behavior, or relationships and of being subjectively somewhat less alien and mysterious than the classical neurotic symptoms have been considered to be.

But if the picture of neurosis and neurotic symptomatology has changed in these general ways, it has certainly not developed with any conceptual clarity or logical cohesion. It appears, rather, that the classical dynamic theory of a dissociated nuclear conflict within the person has merely been stretched to accommodate the more characterological-looking symptoms. The nuclear conflict, which was originally thought to explain the isolated symptom—or, in the theory of self-psychology, the nuclear trauma—is now seen as affecting the person in the somewhat more general ways I indicated.

It is not hard to understand the continued explanatory power of the nuclear-conflict theory. One needs only to be reminded that, as characterological as symptoms may seem, a theory of neurosis—in contrast to a theory of purely adaptive behavior—must still explain a fundamental clinical fact, which the dissociated nuclear conflict conception seems to explain to perfection: the fact of neurotic self-estrangement. That estrangement from one's own wishes, feelings, intentions, or actions may no longer be subjectively as conspicuous as in the case of the classical ego-alien symptom, but it remains the hallmark and the essential meaning of the neurotic conflict and symptom. One person finds herself, not once but regularly, "addicted" to someone she thinks she does not even like; another complains he "cannot" say no and always finds himself "giving in" to others' expectations, though he "doesn't want to"; another person suffers from excruciating indecision "over the simplest things"; another feels intense jealousy that he, himself, calls "insane"; another has "temper" outbursts; still another has a drinking or drug problem that he feels he "cannot" help. These symptoms are not classical ones; they may not be specific or seem mysterious enough to be considered classically ego-alien; and they are not likely to seem isolated from the personality as a whole. But they are reactions that do not seem sensible and may even seem appalling to the one who experiences them; they represent behavior that does not feel freely chosen or intended by its author. How else to explain them, if not as intrusions—even if less sharp and specific ones—of a dissociated nuclear conflict into the rational conscious attitudes of the adult personality? But then we are still left with the basic problems of that conception, now complicated by the picture of symptoms as characterological. What is the role, if any, of the attitudes of consciousness, of the adult personality altogether, in such symptomatic behavior and reactions? What is the relation between an unconscious nuclear conflict, on the one hand, and the attitudes of consciousness, on the other? Are such symptoms consistent with the attitudes of consciousness or are they intrusions?

Heinz Kohut's self-psychology does not escape the problem either. He asserts an essential distinction—none too sharp clinically, in my experience—between symptom neurosis, understood in the classical way of a nuclear drive-defense conflict, on the one hand, and characterological "ego deformity" or "deficiency," on the other.[12] But those supposedly characterological deformities, such as "archaic grandiosity," are at the same time conceived as direct products of childhood trauma, such as a deficient mother-infant relationship, as estranged from the adult personality as a whole ("dissociated from the rest of the psychic apparatus"), and as intrusions into rational adult life ("adult realistic activities . . . are hampered by the breakthrough and intrusion of the archaic structures").[13] The conception is, again, of the patient as directly moved to a behavior or reaction, marionettelike, by the unconscious effects of the early traumatic experience, without apparent reference to the attitudes of consciousness or to the personality as a whole.

Symptomatic Behavior, Consciousness, and Self-Estrangement

The fact is that consciousness does not play as innocuous a role in symptomatic behavior and reaction as the traditional dynamic view suggests. I do not mean that symptoms are consciously designed or chosen, but rather that close observation invariably shows them to be consistent with the attitudes, the ways of thinking, and the sorts of subjective experience that are characteristic of consciousness. It is in this sense that neurotic symptoms may be described as characterological. I am speaking, however, not merely of attitudes and kinds of subjective experience that the individual recognizes or is able to articulate, but of those, articulated or recognized or not, which

---

[12]Kohut, *Analysis of the Self* [11]; see also his *Restoration of the Self* [11].
[13]Kohut, *Analysis of the Self* [11], p. 3.

are *actually* characteristic of him. I am speaking of his characteristic subjective world. Even the strangest symptoms, even those most mystifying to the neurotic person himself, not to speak of less conspicuous and more familiar ones, turn out invariably to be in character, to be consistent with that subjective world, to make sense according to its viewpoint. The conclusion is inescapable, not only that they are not intrusions into that regular world of subjective experience but that they are products of it.

For example, the man who feels compelled to execute certain rituals—procedures that seem utterly meaningless and strange to him as well as to his friends—turns out to be a man who is in general extremely, relentlessly, conscientious. He turns out to be a person who can never allow himself to be satisfied that he has done enough, who therefore does more for the sake of doing more, going through the motions formally, ritualistically.

Yet here—even in this example—is the paradox: On the one hand, there is abundant evidence that the symptom—his compulsive rituals—is in character, absolutely consistent and continuous with his regular attitudes, feelings, and subjective world. On the other hand, there can be no question about his estrangement from himself, from the feelings and ideas that might give subjective meaning to his symptom. In one sense such a symptom is unquestionably alien to its subject; yet in another sense it clearly is not. To put the matter another way, we seem to have a choice between a characterological theory that can explain the consistency of the symptom with the personality as a whole, and a dynamic theory that can explain the estrangement of the symptomatic behavior and reaction from self-awareness.

In a general theoretical way, this dilemma can be solved only by an understanding that is at the same time characterological and dynamic. What is needed is a dynamic understanding, no longer of the dynamics of particular drive and defense but of the working of the personality as a whole. More specifically, the clinical facts seem to point to a neurotic self-estrangement of a different sort from the kind that is usually imagined. It is not an estrangement of a rational adult consciousness from an intrusive, now irrational childhood wish. It is a self-estrangement of a more general kind. It is a distortion or loss of self-awareness, an estrangement of reflective or articulated consciousness from the actuality of a largely unarticulated and diffuse subjective world. To put it more simply, it is an estrangement between what one *thinks* he feels or believes and what he *actually* feels or believes.

A middle-aged man of extremely sensitive pride is rebuffed by his boss. He declares himself to be—he thinks he is— "furious." But he looks far more hurt and humiliated than angry. This unarticulated and diffuse feeling of humiliation is not unconscious, strictly speaking. It is his actual subjective experience. Yet it is unrecognized by him. His pride prevents him from recognizing ("admitting," as he later says) the sensation of humiliation.

A woman, similarly sensitive, is much concerned about her comparatively low professional status and about being "pushed around" by others. She often speaks of herself as a "nobody." She is sincere when she describes herself that way. She is expressing what she thinks she believes, what in fact she often tells herself. But she does not believe it. She does not realize that in fact she constantly disparages her superiors and is contemptuous of them.

Another man constantly and anxiously measures and assures himself of his manliness. He has no awareness at all of the existence of that concern, however. His concern about his manliness continually, but without his notice, prompts him to reassure himself with thoughts about and actions to demonstrate his strong will and his accomplishments. This quasi-reflexive process protects him from awareness of his concern.

These are all instances of self-estrangement, instances in which the individual is cut off from himself. But in each case the estrangement is between the conscious idea of the self, of what one feels, on the one hand, and the actuality of subjective experience, on the other. These are, again, distortions of self-awareness. And they are produced by the internal dynamics of the neurotic personality.

The following is a more extended example. I shall return to it later, in chapter 9, in connection with psychotherapy.

A corporate attorney and teacher of business law in his late forties has been plagued for about six years, since shortly after his second marriage, by the obsessive thought that he has made a terrible mistake in failing to marry another woman, a person he knew only very slightly many years before. His idea is that his life has thereby been irreparably ruined, his chance for happiness missed. This thought, which he calls "crazy," intrudes into his life constantly. He is reminded of this woman and of the idea of his mistake everywhere: almost any popular romantic song, a glimpse of a certain make of car, the mention of the same first name or one that resembles it. Any such associative connection triggers hours of agonized and repetitious review of his supposed mistake and its consequences. He speaks of the obsession as "insane," exasperatedly points out that he hardly knew this woman, and adds, unnecessarily, that in any case no mistake can possibly account for this reaction. Nevertheless, he says, he cannot stop it, cannot "shake it." He sometimes observes that the obsession, if not the supposed mistake, is ruining his life; and in this, of course, one has to agree with him.

To some considerable extent, therefore, this obsessive idea is a subjectively alien symptom, one that is experienced as compulsive, irrational, and painful. Yet it quickly becomes apparent that much the same obsessive quality—or at least the attitudes, the motivations, and the general forms of subjective experience that it comprises—is pervasive in his mental life and that this "insane" obsession is a direct product of them.

This fact is conspicuous, for example, in his business life, which is very successful and occupies a great deal of his interest. He is constantly concerned that he might miss some business opportunity either to learn something of value or to advance his career. He saves and collects great quantities of personal and business records, clippings, newspapers, and magazines and cannot bring himself to throw any of it away, supposedly lest he lose or miss something important. It disturbs him very much to miss a business meeting or professional gathering and he often rushes from one meeting to another. In all of these activities he is driven and oppressed by the concern that the opportunity he is missing or has missed was the most valuable—perhaps even irreplaceable—one.

Despite the fact that such concerns occupy so much of his thought and prompt so much of his activity, he is hardly aware of the existence or nature of the concerns themselves, in contrast to his consciousness of the *objects* of concern, such as the nearly missed meeting. He is unaware of the actual subjective quality of the attitudes and motivations that require these activities—I am speaking primarily of his driven and relentless conscientiousness—and deceives himself about the quality of his experience of the activities themselves. For example, he does not realize that most of the "opportunities" he is so concerned to avoid missing are not experienced by him as opportunities at all, as one can easily judge by his expression. He often tries to sound, and in fact tries to feel, pleased or excited by them; but he does not look pleased or excited. On the contrary, he usually looks dismayed at the discovery of yet another "opportunity," such as a newly announced lecture, and relieved, not disappointed, at the unexpected cancellation of one.

It sometimes happens, for various reasons, that he passes up an "opportunity." At such times, he thinks he feels, and he means to express, feelings of intense frustration and regret. But his feelings are not of regret, for his interest is not essentially in the lost opportunity at all, though he imagines it is; it is in his mistake or his negligence ("Why didn't I . . . !") or its supposed cost. His experience, in other words, is not one of regret but—something quite different—a tortured, actually quite forced, kind of repentance. Indeed, the exaggerated regret that he expresses and the exaggerated value with which he endows missed opportunities do not reflect his actual interest in the loss but *the scrupulousness of his repentance*. This distinction is often confirmed by the fact that when he can persuade himself that he has tried to the extent of his capacity and to the extent that circumstances would allow but has lost an opportunity on account of external factors beyond his control, he is relieved of further remorse.

Altogether he is cut off from any real sense not only of the subjective necessities that give reason to his principal obsessive symptom but equally, or almost so, from those that give reason to much of the rest of his activity. He thinks, and tries to feel, that he wants or is interested in what actually he believes he *should* want or be interested in. He thinks he is interested in a lecture when actually he is interested only in *having been* to the lecture, in having satisfied the requirements of a relentless sense of duty. He thinks he regrets the loss of an opportunity when actually he is repenting the neglect of that duty. All this constitutes a considerable process of self-deception, and it is not merely rationalization that makes this kind of self-deception possible: it is the workings of the dutiful and conscientious attitudes themselves. For although he *experiences* the oppressive effects of that relentless sense of duty, *he is dutiful enough to be persuaded, against strong inner sensation to the contrary, that its requirements are actually his own wishes.*

Thus the operation of certain attitudes of the personality, themselves not consciously articulated, consistently distort self-awareness, as in this patient's scrupulous overvaluation of opportunities, especially missed ones. In the process of such distortion of self-awareness, a self-estrangement is created and the neurotic person is cut off from his own feelings. The result is symptomatic behavior, the aim and reason of which in his subjective life are lost to him.

What then distinguishes this patient's obsessive symptom from so much of the rest of his life and behavior, which bear the same hallmarks? It is obvious that the distinction between what is called symptom and much that is not loses all sharpness. Nevertheless, there is no doubt that the distinctiveness of his symptom was a real one for this patient. It appears that very little remains to account for that distinctiveness apart from its degree. Under certain conditions the restrictive dynamics of the personality—we shall consider this subject further shortly—produces a reaction sufficiently distressing or disruptive to living and a degree of self-estrangement sufficiently extreme to be subjectively conspicuous and not easily rationalized. It is reactions of this subjectively conspicuous sort that neurotic individuals identify as inexplicable symptoms, among all the reactions and behaviors that are products of the same attitudes, that express essentially the same kinds of conflict and self-estrangement, but with which they are long familiar.

The Neurotic Loss of Reality

The workings of neurotic character imply not only some form of estrangement from the self but also some impairment of the experience of objective reality. Various clinical signs of such an impairment are actually well known, but its general significance, and even its general existence, are not. But what else, if not an impaired sense of reality, is reflected in such ordinary neurotic symptoms as obsessive worrying or doubting, or rigid dogmatism, or, more generally, the variety of distortions of relationships that are described as transference reactions? An impaired sense of reality is as intrinsic an aspect of neurotic personality as an impaired or distorted self-awareness. These impairments are, in fact, very closely related, so much so that they should really be considered aspects of a unitary condition. They reflect the two aspects of an impaired differentiation or "polarity," to use Heinz Werner's apt term, between the self and the external world.[14] An understanding of this impairment, as it exists in neurotic conditions, is useful to an understanding of the neurotic person's subjective world and to an understanding of the psychology of therapeutic change as well.

Motivation—wanting this or wanting to do that—or for that matter emotional reactions, feelings in general, do not describe

[14]Heinz Werner, *Comparative Psychology of Mental Development* (Chicago: Follett, 1948).

only internal states; they also describe an individual's relation to the external world, to external objects or figures of interest. And the form or level of conscious articulation of motivation or emotional reaction implies a relation of a certain form or level to the object of interest. Consider the person who wants to do something and knows what he wants to do. He is in a position to plan, to consider his situation and his objective. Actually, it should be put less equivocally: the person who knows he wants to do something cannot avoid planning, considering. His relation to his situation and his goal is an objective, detached one. In this way, the existence of clear and consciously articulated aims and interests implies a detached and objective relation to the objects of those aims or interests, a "polarity" between the self and the external world. This polarity is a developmental achievement. It develops out of an infantile egocentric reactiveness. And it is impaired in one way or another in all psychopathology, neurotic as well as psychotic.

A consequence of the neurotic person's estrangement from his actual feelings or motivations is a reversion to an egocentric reactiveness. In other words, when one does not recognize the existence of one's own interest in a figure or situation, the polarity between oneself and that figure or situation is impaired. That figure or situation is no longer an object of consideration, but a trigger of immediate egocentric reaction.

For example, a man who is neurotically concerned about his dignity and about the possibility of being "pushed around" *and is not aware of these concerns* reacts to a trivial slight with great indignation. He does not see the perpetrator of that slight objectively—in a sense, he does not see *him* at all—but only reacts, out of the unsureness of his respect for himself, to a vague sensation of the other's disrespect. It is much the same when a neurotic person acts in a ritualistic way or is driven by some unarticulated rule. He reacts, say, dutifully, as if signaled by some circumstance—for instance, an "opportunity"—that reminds him anxiously that he "should" do something. He cannot regard that "opportunity" with any objectivity; it is a vague product of the unarticulated press of duty. The process is no less clear in the reaction of an extremely suggestible and intimidated individual to a forceful demand. He reacts with immediate compliance and a vague subjective sensation of "I can't refuse" or "I can't do anything else." Similarly, the intimidated wife, reproached by her husband, cannot regard him with detachment. When he reproaches her, she does not dare even to look at him, certainly not to consider him detachedly. To look at him or think about him with detachment would be to experience herself differently, more completely. Instead, she is absorbed by—almost hypnotized by—the force of his criticism; that criticism is not differentiated from the sensation of her own inadequacy. She speaks of being "criticized" by her husband, but when she says that, she is referring not so much to his behavior as to her insufficiency.

Once aspect of the subject of transference should be noted here, although I shall return to that subject later in the book. The common depiction of transference—as the imposition of a template or image from the past on the present figure of the therapist—does not offer an adequate idea of the actual subjective quality of transference reactions. For it is the nature of such egocentric experiences that they are not sharply defined pictures; they are not objective images with various features misapprehended or distorted. On the contrary, the egocentric image of the other one is not only lacking in sharpness but is, perhaps, hardly an image at all. It is an *experience, a reaction,* compounded of subjective sensation, dimly felt idea, and elements of objective reality fused together. It is also characteristic of such reactions that they and their emotional quality are highly mutable and unstable, precisely for the reason that their emotional quality is not tied to a fixed and objectively regarded figure but to immediate and transitory effects triggered by that figure.

If our understanding is correct, then we may also expect a therapeutic confirmation of the fact. That is, we may expect that as self-estrangement is diminished and the neurotic person comes increasingly into contact with his own feelings, aims, and interests, the polarity between his experience of himself and of the external world will be sharpened. We would expect, in other words, that as self-estrangement is diminished and the neurotic person's own standpoint is clarified for him, the world, viewed from that standpoint, should come into sharper and more objective focus. There is, I believe, ample evidence of such an effect. We shall return to it later.

The Dynamics of Subjective Experience

The existence of restrictive and self-awareness-distorting attitudes—for example, the relentless kind of conscientiousness of the patient described earlier—cannot alone account for the existence of particular symptoms or for their appearance at a particular time. Such attitudes, after all, are more or less continuous and stable; they can account for a fairly continuous self-estrangement or distortion of self-awareness, such as we find in neurotic conditions, but not for the appearance of a particular symptom at a particular time. On the other hand, it would not be correct to imagine that these attitudes or personality styles merely determine the symptomatic form of a conflict that, in another personality, might take another form. It would not be correct, in other words, to imagine that the restrictive attitudes of a particular character merely clothe a certain conflict according to a particular style.

It is true that such attitudes cannot completely explain the symptom because they represent only part of the conflict involved in its production. Nevertheless, they are very much involved in producing that conflict. It is the restrictive reaction of such attitudes to the incipient awareness of certain kinds of feelings and intentions that generates particular forms or kinds of conflict. It is thus impossible to separate the existence of conflict from the existence of these particular forms of it. One cannot say that, in the absence of these particular attitudes, a conflict would take a different form. One can only say that, in the absence of such attitudes, the particular conflict would not exist. Restrictive attitudes, such as obsessively conscientious attitudes, which continuously limit and distort self-awareness, will, under circumstances that further strain their tolerance, give rise to the intensified reactions that we recognize as symptoms. In the case just cited such an intensification and symptomatic exacerbation is evident each time the patient becomes aware of passing up an "opportunity." In other words, each time he consciously, deliberately neglects his duty in order to to follow his own wishes, the patient experiences an intensification of anxiety and an exacerbation of symptoms. In this sense, therefore, the symptom can be said to be the product of the neurotic personality's reaction against itself; it is a product of the dynamics of the personality.

In the neurotic personality, restrictive, largely unarticulated, consciousness-distorting attitudes have developed, such as the rigidly dutiful and conscientious attitudes of obsessive people, or timid and inhibited attitudes, or, in a more specific example, exaggeratedly manly attitudes. We assume that these restrictive and inhibitory attitudes develop originally in order to forestall various kinds of anxiety. Such attitudes tend to exclude certain sorts of feelings and interests from awareness and to trigger inhibitory reactions to any subjective recognition of them. The awareness of oneself feeling certain ways, intending to do, or doing, certain things, even when that awareness is no more than faint or incipient, becomes acutely discomforting. This discomfort, in turn, triggers an intensification of the restrictiveness itself. The result of this reaction is the inhibition of further conscious articulation of the experience and an attenuation or distortion of self-awareness.

Although the workings of these processes are usually very rapid, they can sometimes be easily observed: for example, in obsessive indecision. Obsessively conscientious people, whose life is usually governed by various rules and authoritative principles, often have great difficulty in making decisions that rest inescapably on personal preference. They can easily make choices that can be settled, or can seem to be settled, on the basis of some technical information—where there is or appears to be a "right" answer. But they may be thrown into anxiety by even inconsequential decisions when there is no rule or authority to refer to. It can easily be observed of these people that, precisely at the moment that they become aware of leaning toward a choice, they experience anxiety, often in the form of a sense of recklessness or impetuousness ("I might be making a mistake!"). This anxiety, in turn, characteristically prompts an intensified and scrupulous review of the choice. More precisely, it prompts a scrupulous review of all adverse arguments and facts: a biased review, scrupulous only in the cautionary direction.

To a dutiful person of this sort, who lives with a constant

awareness of what he "should" do, the sensation of making a decision on the basis of no higher authority than his own personal choice or judgment is bound to feel audacious. It is true—and significant—that such a person continually makes decisions of this kind, as we all do, without noticing them and therefore without discomfort. But some decisions call attention to themselves, often merely because they are not routine, not necessarily because they involve important consequences. They cannot be made without a subjective awareness of choosing. That awareness of making a personal choice or judgment contains (as anyone can easily experience by making the experiment in imagination) an attitude of freedom and a sensation of one's own authority that are quite different from and actually inimical to the attitudes of the dutiful follower of rules, the good soldier. These are the occasions of decision that give rise to acute discomfort. They do so primarily not because of what the choices symbolize but because of how choosing feels.

A dutiful and conscientious person who feels momentarily reckless or impetuous becomes more conscientious and dutiful. He does not think about reacting this way; it is the only way he can react. The discomforting awareness of an intention to make a choice will trigger a corrective intensification of that conscientiousness. In the case of obsessive indecision the scrupulous, cautionary respect paid selectively to those facts or arguments adverse to one's inclination of the moment—whatever that inclination may be—results, finally, in a state of confusion, in the loss of a sense of the whole. Instead, there are only inconclusive data, pros and cons, selective lists of features that can be read at one moment one way, the next moment another way. It is at such a point that obsessive people will often say, "I don't know what I want!" The corrective intensification of the conscientious attitude in reaction to an incipient choice has inhibited the further development of awareness of choice. In other words, the process has distorted self-awareness and has produced a state of neurotic self-estrangement, and a symptom.

Similar dynamics operate in every neurotic condition in a rapid, subjectively unnoticed, and largely unarticulated way. Evidence of these processes may, however, be observable externally.

For example, a sensitive and defensive and, therefore, often angry woman is tempted to forgive a friend who has treated her badly. She is tempted to "let her off the hook." It is apparent that, perhaps in spite of herself, she likes this person. She is tempted to allow herself to relax her accustomed and principled militancy in such matters and in that sense to let herself, as well as her friend, off the hook. It is apparent that this temptation is discomforting to her, however, because before it is even completely articulated the idea abruptly "occurs" to her that a resumption of friendly relations would be to make "a doormat" of herself. This anxious thought of indignity is triggered by the sensation of relaxing her accustomed guardedness. The thought, in turn, leads immediately to a review of several other instances of victimization, and her angry resolve is rearoused. She now concludes that to forgive "would be hypocrisy."

Her anger, as one who observes her realizes, is actually somewhat forced, worked up. She goads herself, without realizing that she is doing so, with the humiliating thought that she has been a "doormat" in the past when she has forgiven such things and would be again. She thinks she should feel, she tries to feel, and believes she does feel angrier than she really is. This process also, therefore, is one that distorts self-awareness.

Another patient, a timid woman in her early fifties, is usually quite mindful of her own unimportance. She is, accordingly, much concerned with being "nice," that is, with satisfying others' expectations. On a particular occasion, she momentarily forgets her accustomed concern and reacts to someone's unreasonable demand with annoyance. When she becomes aware of her own reaction, she immediately feels "inconsiderate" and "selfish." That anxious and abhorrent experience of herself signals the beginning of a corrective reaction. Her anxiety reflexively triggers an intensified and corrective consciousness of herself from the standpoint of others.

An anxious reaction of this sort to the awareness of one's own feelings or actions cannot be thought to reflect merely an associative significance attached to the particular event, such as an associative connection to a childhood prototype. It is not only that reactions of this sort are too general, too much reactions to *kinds* of self-awareness for such explanations. It is also that such explanations are not subjective enough; they are too peripheral to the personality of the individual involved, when it is obvious that the individual's personality is the decisive factor in the reaction. The awareness, perhaps even the dim, unarticulated sensation, of doing a certain sort of thing or of having a certain sort of reaction will bring with it a sensation of the self that will be congenial to a person of one personality, discomforting to another, and abhorrent to a third. In general, self-awareness of a particular kind will be abhorrent, will trigger first a characteristic form of anxiety and then a corrective reaction, in a specific personality, if it is actually inimical to the existing attitudes of the personality.

The subjective reaction to particular intentions or actions will depend not so much on the objective nature of those actions as on the attitude which they embody. Thus the same action may trigger anxiety in an individual when it is done with one attitude, but not when done with another. With a different attitude, the same action may involve quite a different kind of self-awareness. Thus, a "manly" man can comfortably tell a woman he loves her if he knows that he does not mean it but cannot do so when he does mean it, even if he does not realize that he does mean it.

An aspect of the famous case of the paranoid Schreber, to which I referred earlier, offers an interesting example of this point. Early in his psychosis, the rigidly upright and moralistic Schreber was acutely alarmed, even frantic, at the sensation that he was being "unmanned" and his will undermined by the insinuation of female "nerves" into his body. It is clear from his *Memoirs,* however, that Schreber's panic was a reaction not merely to the homosexual impulse as such, but to a whole sexual attitude and sensation of himself as wanton and voluptuous, which he identified as female.[15] This is apparent in the fact that later, though still paranoid, Schreber became much calmer and actually reconciled himself to the idea of his female sexuality, including its voluptuousness, when he saw it in a new light. For he developed the idea that it was his *duty* to serve God sexually in this way. Thus, the sexual transformation that had initially been abhorred as destructive of his honor and dignity was now experienced with a different attitude, gave rise to a different kind of self-awareness, and could be accepted.[16]

The general process in which the personality reacts against certain of its own tendencies can be described as the way in which, at some cost, the neurotic personality maintains its stability and is in that respect self-regulating. The personality reacts quasi-reflexively and correctively, prompted by anxiety or

[15]Schreber, *Memoirs* [6].
[16]See Shapiro, *Autonomy and Rigid Character* [4], pp. 146ff., for a more complete discussion of the case.

shame or some other acute discomfort, to sensations or kinds of awareness of the self that threaten its stability or are inimical to its present form, usually before they are more than faint or incipient. In this sense, the restrictive and self-awareness-distorting attitudes of the neurotic personality operate to maintain stability not only in a corrective way but also in a preventive way; not only to dispel but also to forestall anxiety.

A restrictive personality of this sort is more or less continuously in a state of tension, inasmuch as a relaxation of its restrictiveness will, at a certain threshold of self-awareness, generate anxiety and trigger a corrective reaction. Hence there is also, more or less continuously, a degree of distortion of self-awareness or self-deception associated with such a personality. Actually, we are familiar from clinical experience with such continuous self-deceptions. The exaggerated manliness of one; the exaggeratedly "female" cuteness of another; the continual, somewhat forced gloom of the worrier; the artificial, self-conscious dignity of the prideful; and so forth all involve more or less stable forms of such restrictive and self-awareness-distorting tension. Each of these conditions also involves a degree of accustomed anxiety and largely unarticulated self-conscious concern: one person will often be on the edge of a sensation of shame or humiliation; another will always have a vague, nagging sense that he should have done more or should have done less; another will be quick to note that he is not liked.

It may be asked whether neurotic character invariably involves such tension and internal conflict. In some neurotic individuals, tension and conflict of this sort are obvious, as in compulsive people continually wrestling with themselves; or rigidly "manly" men clearly concerned—though they may not realize it—about being weak. But in many individuals whom

43

NEUROTIC CHARACTER AND PSYCHOTHERAPY

one would not hesitate to describe as neurotic, at least in an approximate sense, internal conflict and self-estrangement are not so evident. One might reasonably think that the problem in these cases is not internal conflict but a more or less stable distortion or deficiency of the personality. It is not that these individuals—for example, some extremely passive or extremely timid and suggestible individuals—seem comfortable, but that their distress appears to be derived not from internal conflict as much as from conflict, or at least trouble, with the external world.

For example: A housewife in her early thirties is, it seems clear, browbeaten by her husband, some fifteen years older. He tells her that she is inadequate as a wife, sexually and otherwise uninteresting, and incompetent in running the house. It appears, as she tells her story, that there is no question of her psychological distress or of the existence of psychopathology: she is not only quite depressed but, in her evident acceptance of her husband's evaluation of her, she seems remarkably impressionable, almost brainwashed. His caustic descriptions of her appear to be accepted and repeated by her literally. It is not merely that his words continue to come to mind, but that they seem to come to mind not as *his* words but, now, as hers. She evidently thinks of herself through his eyes, with his language; yet it seems that she has little awareness that it is his language and his view. Her sense of her own authority seems to be severely diminished. She seems to feel so lacking in qualifications and authority as to be disqualified from holding any independent opinions or point of view.

There can hardly be a question that this kind of impressionability, though not rare, reflects psychopathology. But where is the evidence of internal conflict and tension? Indeed, the patient's distress seems plainly to be a product not of her relationship with herself but of her relationship with her husband, and specifically her failure to satisfy him. She comes to a therapist, after all, out of *that* distress, to be "improved" according to her husband's definition, to be made a "more interesting" person.

The internal conflict and tension are, however, not hard to find. The evidence of such conflict is located, as it always is, close to the evidence of self-estrangement. The conflict appears, for example, when we notice that the patient's attitude about what her husband has said is not absolutely consistent. For example, although she talks about herself and her situation predominantly from her husband's point of view, as if it were her own, occasionally there are noticeable, if small, lapses. Speaking of her handling of money, she says, *"He* says. . . ." When she speaks in this way, presenting his views not simply as fact but with the particular emphasis of *"He* says," a slightly different attitude is implied, even if she is not aware of it. However much she may indicate her agreement—even if she does not consider it necessary to indicate her agreement— there appears to be at least a dim awareness that his point of view is, after all, *his* point of view.

In such a small awareness, the neurotic schism and conflict are expressed. That intimation (*"He* says . . .") informs us, even if she does not realize it, that the view she usually expresses does not wholly represent her subjective experience, that another view exists, and that the two contend, if as yet quietly, for expression. One notices, then, that the voice she uses when she represents her husband's views is an artificial voice. It is not a voice of conviction; it sounds unhappy, but in some way stilted or rote, perhaps like the voice of a child reciting a lesson. She evidently must forestall any inclination to speak in her own voice.

It is inevitable that such a schism and conflict should exist.

The picture of a brainwashed person, without opinions or a point of view of her own, is not a complete picture of any person. Human beings are thinking creatures, even if they might prefer not to be. They are as much thinking creatures, barring grave physical damage, as they are breathing creatures. They cannot avoid awareness of their own judgment or their own view of things for a long period of time without tension or effort of some kind. In a person who is intimidated as this person is, without respect for and even largely without awareness of her own judgment, the very existence of that judgment will be inimical to her timidity. The fleeting awareness of her own dissenting judgment, even the sensation of doubt or of inattention to her husband's views, will generate anxiety, a vague sense of going beyond her qualifications, of presumption, of abandoning reliable authority; and it will trigger a corrective reaction.

It is true that this person is hardly if at all aware of that internal conflict, whereas she is acutely aware of her apprehension and misery in relation to the external situation (when, for example, she must face her husband's displeasure). She is hardly aware of the existence of internal conflict precisely for the reason that a corrective reaction that forestalls the conscious development of that experience is triggered in its incipient stages. This state of affairs is, in fact, the general rule in psychopathology. What we see clinically is not so much anxiety and internal conflict as the avoidance of them, usually through more or less continuously sustained inhibitory reactions, which diminish or distort self-awareness. Thus, this patient shrinks from awareness of her own judgment or of any doubts of her husband's authority. She tries to keep herself "in her place," on the whole, attentive to his every word, mindful of her own inadequacies, concerned only to be satisfactory to him. And that problem, of being satisfactory to him, which reveals her internal conflict only in its momentary pauses and hesitations, is the problem that she presents to the therapist.

One might think that if such an exaggerated and painful humility is required to forestall the anxiety of internal conflict, then the patient suffers more from the medicine than from the original illness. But such reactions, of course, are not calculated and involve no choice; the inhibitory reaction occurs essentially reflexively and without conscious awareness. As miserable as she may feel when her husband tells her how inadequate she is, she nevertheless automatically shrinks in discomfort from any doubts about his judgment. In the sense that this case illustrates, any neurotic style forestalls or diminishes the experience of anxiety and internal conflict by inhibiting and restricting function—in the case described, by inhibiting self-assertion, initiative, and independent judgment. Other functions, of course, may be overdeveloped.

The workings of this dynamics of the personality to which subjective experience and sensation are so central are not themselves spontaneously accessible to awareness. The reason is not hard to understand in a general way. These are processes of self-deception: their result is a loss of self-awareness and therefore of awareness of the very fact that such a loss has occurred. Hence the processes are essentially invisible to their subjects. The exaggeratedly manly man who stiffens defensively at the faintest sensation or idea that he is too sentimental or soft cannot be aware of that process. He cannot because at that first anxious dim sensation, before the concern has become fully articulated, he will feel prompted to do something tough, something that diminishes his anxiety and reassures him of his manliness. Indeed, it is apparent that to become aware of such self-deception is to begin its undoing—a fact of obvious therapeutic significance.

These consciousness-distorting and consciousness-attenuating processes can also be described as performing the essential function of the traditional defense mechanisms. That is, they prevent certain sorts of ideas, feelings, and motivations—not merely particular ideas or impulses, but whole classes of subjective experience—from achieving full conscious articulation or self-awareness. The traditionally recognized defense mechanisms, the list and definition of which have long been recognized as unsystematic, seem to be special instances of the workings of such restrictive processes in particular personalities.[17] The defense mechanism of projection, for example— which otherwise has been little understood psychologically— can be understood as a corrective intensification of a certain kind of rigid defensiveness. For instance, a rigid and exaggerated manliness may, under conditions of special tension, become defensively sensitive and finally, if defensive enough, projective.[18]

In the traditional psychoanalytic conception, however, the processes of defense—as well as the feelings, wishes, and thoughts they are directed against—have been considered to be essentially unconscious. Only the results of the defense process—of projection, reaction formation, and such—and various derivatives of the wishes or anxieties that are involved in the process are thought to be present in conscious experience, where they are considered of no further dynamic significance. Indeed, the relation of the defense mechanisms to the psychology of consciousness as a whole has not been a matter of great psychoanalytic interest in the past. Defense mechanisms have usually been treated as more or less elementary unconscious devices; often they are referred to as being "used" by the person. The self-awareness-distorting processes which I have described as fulfilling the functions of defense, by contrast, are

[17]See Shapiro, *Neurotic Styles* [1].
[18]See Shapiro, *Autonomy and Rigid Character* [4], pp. 140ff.

general psychological processes and reactions *of* the person. They are not "conscious" in the sense of being consciously articulated or reflectively conscious, and certainly they are not deliberate. But they are processes and reactions of the personality that are regulated by subjective experience and sensation, by unarticulated, dimly conscious sensations and ideas of the self. Such a conception of defense—as an automatic consciousness- or self-awareness-distorting reaction of the personality— seems closer to the clinical facts than the traditional concept, based on a quasi-mechanical model of an energy or drive-controlling structure.

I do not wish to suggest that the entire neurotic personality is contained within the content of subjective experience or its dynamics at a particular time. In a military conflict, the troops ranged in a particular battle do not constitute the whole of the forces involved in the conflict; it is not a personal battle between two gangs of men. The particular battle embodies and has been brought into existence by the relation of larger tendencies or forces to each other; it is, under the particular circumstances, their immediate point of contact. Similarly, the internal conflict within subjective experience has been brought into existence by the *conflict-generating* organization of the personality, the workings of its restrictive style, in the particular circumstances. It is in this organization, in its general forms of experience and internal schemas, its action patterns, its reaction tendencies, its dispositions and attitudes—and in the memories and experiences that have been assimilated to them—that childhood history has its influence, rather than in the content of particular memories. It is this organization, also, that may be described as largely unconscious.[19]

[19]This conception of the unconscious follows that proposed, as compatible with contemporary psychological findings, by Jean G. Schimek in "A Critical Re-exami-

The distinction I am drawing, between a dynamics of the neurotic personality or character and a dynamics of a nuclear conflict that acts on the personality, is not a pedantic distinction. It has extensive implications for therapeutic work. As will become clear in part two, for example, the distinction implies a significant difference in the direction of therapeutic attention, that is, in the understanding of what constitutes the therapeutic material.

nation of Freud's Concept of Mental Representation," *International Review of Psychoanalysis* 2 (1975): 171.

PART TWO

The Therapeutic
Material

Chapter 3

The Words and the Speaker

What Is the Therapeutic Material?

It is usual in psychotherapy for the therapist to encourage, if not require, the patient to reveal himself, to speak freely about himself, particularly about his problems and his innermost feelings. I am not referring merely to the initial information that a therapist may request, but to a continuing expectation. The purest example of this expectation, of course, is the "basic rule" of psychoanalysis, which asks of the patient that he suspend his usual critical judgment and say without censorship whatever enters his mind. The general aim of this method is not ambiguous. It is to penetrate the superficial, the purely rational and consciously recognized, and to gain or improve access to the essential subject matter of the therapy, the therapeutic material, the expressions or reflections of the underlying neurotic problems or conflicts. It is assumed that this material must be provided in this way by the patient, that it requires his cooperation to this extent, and that it can be found in what he provides. It is understood that this material is likely to be disturbing or painful to the patient, and the patient's inability or refusal to comply with these procedures—sometimes deliberate, in the more interesting instances not—is well recognized as resistance.

The logic of these procedures and their view of the therapeutic material seems at first to be quite clear and unarguable, even obvious. Yet it is not in actuality unarguable and has not been so at least from the time of the early psychoanalytic interest in the ego, perhaps even from the time of Freud's abandonment of the preanalytic method of hypnosis in favor of psychoanalysis proper.

In those early days of the trauma theory of neurosis, the definition of the therapeutic material was completely clear: it was the memory of the repressed trauma. The techniques of hypnosis and then of guided associations were directly aimed at gaining access to that material. However, with the enlargement of Freud's interest beyond traumatic memories and the recognition of more intrinsic causes and a more complicated fabric of neurosis, the implied definition of the therapeutic material necessarily became much broader and at the same time less precise. For now it was recognized that derivatives of and associative links to the infantile conflict might appear in the patient's productions in any connection. Hence the method of free association and the basic rule, the requirement to omit nothing, in order to gain access to those derivatives and associative links. But it is when psychoanalytic interest shifts its emphasis to the study of the ego and includes interest not only in what is repressed but also in the agencies of repression that a significant ambiguity appears in the definition of therapeutic material. For at this point, therapeutic interest includes not only the infantile wish- and fantasy-linked associations and memories that the basic rule was designed to make accessible, but also the nature of the various kinds of resistance to their emergence and to following the basic rule itself. Theoretically, the definition of the therapeutic material has changed; it includes not just what lies behind the defensive processes but the defensive processes themselves. Yet the continued use of the basic rule, as well as the custom of the patient lying on the couch, clearly retain, albeit in a compromised form, something of the very effort to circumvent the ego, which was the original value but ultimately the deficiency of hypnosis. That effort seems still to imply that what lies *behind* the defensive processes is the real material.

Anna Freud addresses the problem in her classic work, *The Ego and the Mechanisms of Defense*. She says, "The fundamental rule can never be followed beyond a certain point." She means by this that the existence of the ego implies an unavoidable opposition to the strivings of the id for expression. Underscoring the point, she says that if, indeed, it were possible, as "many beginners" believe, to induce the patient to give all of his associations without inhibition or modification, "it would not represent an advance, for after all it would simply mean the conjuring up again of the now obsolete situation of hypnosis, with its one-sided concentration on the part of the physician upon the id."[1]

Why not, then, abandon this rule? The answer given is that

[1] Anna Freud, *The Ego and the Mechanisms of Defense*, rev. ed., vol. II of *The Writings of Anna Freud* (1936; reprint, New York: International Universities Press, 1966), p. 13.

the partial suspension of the ego which can be achieved not only permits the emergence of ideational derivatives of unconscious impulses (fantasies, memories, and so forth) to some degree but also brings into sharp relief the ego's resistance to that emergence. Thus, both kinds of material, the derivative contents of unconscious impulses and the resistance to those impulses, will be elicited. But this answer is not completely satisfactory. Its point may be granted if the expression of the neurotic conflict—the therapeutic material—is limited to such ideational content and the resistance against it. If, however, those attitudes, ways, interests, and purposes that are suspended in compliance with the basic rule are also parties to the neurotic conflict, then Anna Freud's argument comparing compliance with that rule to the obsolete use of hypnosis can be directed in lesser degree against this suspension of the ego as well. In short, the ego was now recognized in principle as therapeutic material of equal status to that of derivatives of the repressed impulses, but in practice the effort to circumvent the ego was not completely abandoned.

Actually, the shift in the conception of the nature of the therapeutic material had, by the time Anna Freud wrote these words, already taken a more radical form in Wilhelm Reich's "character analysis."[2] Reich argued that the primary defense against unconscious impulses, and therefore the primary resistance against their reexperience in psychoanalytic therapy, consists of the patient's neurotic character. He described this character as comprising various generalized, individually characteristic attitudes, forms of behavior, and "ways of being" (submissive, haughty, conventionally polite, ironic, etc.), ways which were, we judge from his description, essentially artificial

[2]Wilhelm Reich, *Character Analysis* (New York: Orgone Institute Press, 1949). The essential material was originally presented in 1927.

and defensive and which cut the neurotic person off from the experience of his own feelings, drives, and anxieties. Thus the same dynamic content—in his example, hatred of the analyst—will be covered in one case by an exaggerated submissiveness and in another by defensive haughtiness. Only through the prior analysis, the "lifting," of these defensive attitudes and ways, Reich insisted, would effective interpretation and reexperience of the underlying feelings and impulses be possible, even if the content of what the patient said might seem to offer opportunity for earlier interpretation. Reich formulated his view in an instruction to the therapist that is directly aimed at revising the understanding of the therapeutic material: "The *how* of saying things is as important 'material' for interpretation as is *what* the patient says" (original emphasis).[3]

The Patient Is the Therapeutic Material

Reich's recommendation—pay attention to *how* the patient talks—is a very powerful one. It is far more radical in its redirection of the therapist's attention than, say, any of the proposals, not rare in psychiatric history, for this or that revision of the nature or developmental stage of a nuclear conflict. Reich's recommendation is not merely to look for something different in what the patient provides; it is not merely another proposal for a different analysis of the same text. Instead, it points the therapist's attention in a new direction, no longer only to what the patient provides, but to the patient, the person. I propose to emphasize that point by paraphrasing

[3]Ibid., p. 45.

Reich's principle as follows: Pay attention not only to the *words* but also to the *speaker*. The patient, not merely what the patient provides, is the therapeutic material.

Actually, the nature of Reich's interest in the way the patient talks was limited by his theoretical premises, his one-sided and schematic conception of neurotic "character" as a restrictive institution—inhibiting, blocking, resisting the healthy discharge of affect and drive energy. When Reich spoke of paying attention to "how the patient talks," he referred to the way the patient talks *in general,* to the characteristic manner and "way of being" that regularly inhibits this discharge and wards off feelings and feeling-charged memories. In his conception, therefore, the general character resistance, the patient's manner (obedient, aggressive, polite, etc.) was to be addressed first; then, especially "in the later stages," the content of early experience.[4]

But actually, how the patient talks has both a more far-reaching and a more specific significance than as an overall restrictive form. Everything that is said is said in one way or another. And everything that is said is said in a specific way for specific and immediate reasons, which are sometimes known to the speaker, but often not. To pay attention to the way something is said or to the attitude with which it is said, therefore, is to enlarge understanding of its immediate significance for the speaker, to enlarge understanding beyond the abstract textual meaning of the words to the immediate use to which they are being put. It is often, in fact, to see the dynamics of the speaker in action.

In the following example, the therapist notices the peculiar way in which a patient talks about a matter on her mind. A

young woman tells a story about a confrontation with her
boyfriend: they had an argument on the telephone about some
behavior of his. She says emphatically that what he did was
outrageous, and she describes the event and her outrage—she
hung up indignantly. She starts the story at the beginning of
the conversation and goes through every step—he said, I said,
and so on. The therapist becomes aware that the story has
become rather tedious; it sounds somewhat like court testi-
mony. The point, however, is not to hurry her up. She must
have her reasons for telling the story in this way, though the
therapist does not understand them, and very likely she does
not know them either at this point.

> THERAPIST *(interrupts):* Excuse me, but I wonder why you
> tell me all the details so carefully.
> PATIENT: Well . . . I don't know . . . I want you to get a
> picture of exactly what happened.
> THERAPIST: You think I might get the wrong idea?
> PATIENT *(laughs, confused):* Well . . . well . . . *he* says I threw
> a tantrum!
> THERAPIST: Perhaps you are not so sure he was wrong.
> PATIENT *(again laughs, confused; her voice becomes quieter):*
> Well . . . I . . . I did, I guess. . . . No, I didn't! . . . I don't
> know . . . I guess I did. . . . And now I don't know what
> to do.

In other words, this patient is not, as she thinks, simply
telling a story of her boyfriend's outrageous behavior. She is
making a case, reviewing the evidence and trying to put to rest
certain doubts she has—though at the moment not clearly
aware that she has—about her own behavior and his charges.
And this effort, prompted by that dim but uncomfortable

sensation of doubt about her innocence, is represented in how she talks about the incident. Actually, one can say more than that. The effort to dispel her doubt is not merely *represented* in how she tells the story; that effort is actually *continued* in how she tells the story.

The principle, The patient, not merely what the patient provides, is the therapeutic material, and its attendant recommendation, Pay attention not only to the words but also to the speaker, have many ramifications. Thus, it is apparent that from this standpoint one cannot speak of an absence of material or of a patient producing more material or less material. If the material consists of the patient, not of what the patient produces, it is present in its entirety as soon as the patient enters the room.

For example, a very prideful, self-conscious man, who cannot stand the indignity, as it seems to him, of being a patient or admitting "weakness," enters the office and walks to the window with an artificial manner of self-confidence. He talks about the weather, the view, the football scores, all in the manner of man to man, all without genuine interest. Yet this behavior is not an absence of therapeutic material. It *is* the material—his forced self-confidence, his artificiality, his effort to be the therapist's equal because, without knowing it, he feels himself to be less.

In another example, a severely obsessional young man enters the office, sits down, and after silently but visibly agonizing for a few minutes says, "I can't decide where to start." From his standpoint of assuming that he *provided* the material, his statement was quite sensible. But from the therapist's standpoint he had already started, silently, on entering, with characteristic worry and indecision about "where to start."

The same principles also direct the therapist's attention

unambiguously to the present, the "here and now." The patient, in contrast to what the patient talks about, always exists in the present. It is only when the therapist limits his attention to what the patient is saying—to the text or the narrative content—and overlooks the speaker that the therapist's interest is likely to be drawn away from what is immediately relevant.

In comparison with the principle, Pay attention not only to the words but also to the speaker, the frequently heard therapeutic recommendation to attend to the "here and now" seems vague and ambiguous, for there are several possible interpretations of that recommendation. It is sometimes understood to mean that the patient's allusions to figures outside the therapy are to be interpreted as metaphors for or displaced references to the therapist. This understanding reflects an effort to find immediate significance in the therapeutic material, but it looks for that significance only in the narrative content of what the patient says, where it is not necessarily to be found at all. Actually, the "here and now" recommendation should not be taken to mean that what the patient says necessarily refers to his immediate circumstances. It means, rather, that the patient must have *a present reason* for saying what he says, whatever it refers to.

For example, the person who carries a grudge, who is obsessed with an old injustice or defeat and can talk of nothing else, does so for present reasons. He feels, perhaps, that to allow the recollection of that defeat to fade, without evening the score, is to resign himself to it, to take it lying down, and therefore to be further humiliated. What he talks about is old, but these feelings about it are, of course, in the present. And the dynamics of these present feelings is reflected in the way he talks about it now.

Saying Something Is Doing Something

The distinction between *what* is said and *how* it is said calls our attention not only to the existence of a speaker but, specifically, to the relation between the speaker and what he says. Speech, such as our patients' speech, does not consist only of text: it consists of text employed by a person. Linguistic philosophers refer, therefore, to "speech acts" or "utterances."[5] Speech is, in other words, an action, an action with a point, with some degree of intentionality. To borrow from J. L. Austin: *Saying something is doing something.*[6] The same text may be employed in different ways to have one or another meaning or point, and its statement may constitute one or another kind of speech act. For example, the statement "I'll be back this afternoon" may be a warning, or it may be a promise. "Why did you do that?" may be a question or, more likely, a reproach.

If the text or speech content is employed by the speaker in a speech act or utterance, then we can say that the point of that utterance is generally reflected in *how* it is said. That is one way we determine whether the spoken statement "I'll be back this afternoon" is a promise or a warning. How something is said— in written language this is generally established by context and punctuation, in addition to style—is the way we determine the relation of the speaker to the words he is using, the use to which he puts his words, the aim or point of his utterance. This can be seen in the simple case of my examples, in which the speaker presumably is consciously aware of his point, to prom-

[5]See J. L. Austin, *How to Do Things with Words* (Cambridge, Mass.: Harvard University Press, 1962). Also, John R. Searle, *Expression and Meaning: Studies in the Theory of Speech Acts* (Cambridge, Eng.: Cambridge University Press, 1979).

[6]See Austin, *How to Do Things with Words* [5], esp. pp. 94ff.

ise or to threaten or to reproach; and it is equally true of the more complicated case—I shall give examples shortly—in which the speaker is estranged from the nature or even the existence of his aims.

The speech act can be quite deliberate and consciously purposeful, of course, as in giving careful instructions or telling a lie or making a promise; or it can be relatively spontaneous, its communicative aims unnoticed and taken for granted, as in normal conversation; or, for that matter, it can be deliberately and purposefully "spontaneous," as in trying to follow the basic rule of psychoanalysis. In any case, the aims of speech are usually social ones, communicative ones—it is a social kind of action—to inform, amuse, prompt action, express affection, and so forth. But sometimes the aims of speech are not primarily social or communicative ones at all, though they may be assumed to be. Sometimes the purpose of speech is not so much to communicate with another person as to affect the speaker himself.[7] The speech act may be, in other words, not so much an expression of the individual's relationship with another person as an expression of his momentary relationship with himself. It may be, in fact, less an expression of his thoughts or feelings than an unrecognized reaction against them, an effort to dispel or revise them. Speech then becomes a continuation of the dynamics of self-deception. For this reason the aims of such speech are intrinsically unrecognizable to the subject himself.

Consider the example of compulsive people, people who live with a more or less constant sense of unfulfilled responsibilities concerning what they should do and feel, even what they

[7]Compare Jean Piaget's concept of "egocentric speech" in his *Language and Thought of the Child,* trans. Marjorie Gabain (1926; reprint, New York: The Humanities Press, 1952).

should be. Very often their awareness of such duties and responsibilities and their ambivalence about them prompt these people to silent, but oppressive, nagging reproaches, warnings, and reminders to themselves. This nagging—which is largely unrecognized by them, though they both do it and experience its oppressive effects—is also very often evident in the way they talk.[8]

Thus, statements that might easily seem from a textual standpoint to be simple statements of intention or communications of fact, such as "I really want to move. I don't know why I don't do anything about it. I know it would be good for me" or "I have to get that review done tomorrow," are, in actual speech, uttered with an emphasis that gives them a special urgency. It is as if they end with exclamation marks. They are imperatives: "I really want to move! I don't know why I don't do anything about it! I know it would be good for me!" or "I have to get the review done tomorrow!" These statements mean, of course, "I *should* move! I should have moved already!" or "I may have jeopardized my position by putting off the review!"

The same urgent, admonishing, angrily reproachful manner is evident in the example I mentioned earlier of a woman speaking about a relationship of hers of which she disapproves. She begins with a rhetorical question; obviously it is no question but an imperative: "What's the *matter* with me? I've got to end this thing! There's nothing in it for me!" Another patient repents his eating habits with a reproachful warning: "I've got to stop eating so much! It's killing me!"

These statements are not primarily communications to another but admonitions, warnings, reproaches of the speaker to

[8]See David Shapiro, "Speech Characteristics of Rigid Characters," *Language and Style* 10, no. 4 (1977): 262–69.

himself—anxious corrective reactions to a sense of neglect or transgression of duty. That fact explains both their stridency and their typical exaggerations for greater effect ("It's killing me!"). For all their stridency, these self-reproaches by no means necessarily imply intention to reform. They often promise reform, in the way of acts of contrition, but the promise is not wholehearted.

Speech such as I have shown in these examples—supposedly communicative but actually more or less directly self-addressed—is particularly characteristic of the dynamics of obsessive-compulsive individuals. There are various other sorts of slightly less direct self-address (for example, "I know I did the right thing!") and many kinds of speech in which the speaker is not addressing himself with any directness at all that are nevertheless aimed primarily not at communicating with another person but at affecting the speaker himself. In all of these instances, speech is a distortion, not a communication, of consciousness.

Thus, when a patient tells a story with artificial enthusiasm or brightness or conviction, or with an exaggerated toughness, or artificial cuteness; or when he tries to make a case, to persuade the other of something he, himself, wants to believe, thinks he believes, but does not believe ("She told me she loves me, and I'm *sure* she means it"); or when he rails against his boss, as though making a speech—in all of these instances he is, without recognizing the fact, not so much concerned with communicating with another person as he is talking for his own ear. In all of these cases the words are not so much an expression of a feeling or conviction as they are used in an effort to create or dispel some feeling or conviction.

Hellmuth Kaiser was the first to describe clearly the characteristic forced or artificial quality of the neurotic person's expression of his own thoughts or feelings and to point out its central pathological and therapeutic significance.[9] He said succinctly that a general symptom of neurosis is that "the patient does not talk straight" or that he is not completely "behind" his words.[10] What the patient says is not "straightforward self-expression."[11] We may add that the neurotic person does not "talk straight" because he thinks he feels, he tries to feel, something different from what he actually feels. His speech, moreover, does not merely reflect that self-deception and distortion of self-awareness. The utterances I have described are *self-deceptive speech acts*. The speech acts themselves, prompted by some unrecognized anxiety, are part of the process of self-deception and distortion of self-awareness.

One other striking feature of this kind of speech should be noted. It reflects the diminished polarity, of which I spoke earlier, in the neurotic person's experience of himself and the other. When a person talks in the ways I have indicated by these examples, he is essentially his own audience, and the other person becomes for him only a further means of registering an effect or confirming a point. When, for instance, the patient loudly and forcefully makes an assertion ("I know it would be good for me!"), half-believing himself to have an enthusiasm and conviction that he does not have, he is not talking *to* the therapist. He may look at the therapist's face fixedly; perhaps he will search there for a confirming signal; but his interest is essentially inward, in his own utterance, not in communication with the other. Indeed, the very loudness and

---

[9]Hellmuth Kaiser, "The Problem of Responsibility in Psychotherapy," and "The Universal Symptom of the Psychoneuroses: A Search for the Conditions of Effective Psychotherapy," both in *Effective Psychotherapy: The Contribution of Hellmuth Kaiser*, ed. L. B. Fierman (New York: Free Press, 1965), pp. 1–13, 14–171.

[10]Kaiser, "Universal Symptom" [9], p. 36.

[11]Kaiser, "Problem of Responsibility" [9], p. 4.

forcefulness with which he speaks is a reflection of that fact, for the tone and volume of his voice are not adjusted, as they otherwise would be, for communication with another person at that distance. Accordingly, the therapist will not experience genuine contact with the patient at such moments. We will return in chapter 7 to the therapeutic significance of this fact.

Two Pictures of the Patient

We may listen to a patient in two ways. We may listen to language and we may listen to speech. Language—a narrative, say, told by our patient—generally has a referent; it is about something. This referent—what it is about—is what we mean by its content, its text, or by "what" it says. At the same time, as speech it is an action by a person employing that content. I have introduced the concept of the speech act here because, when recognized as a speech act, the patient's narrative tells us not only about its subject matter (its referent) but also about the speaker as he is, with us, at that moment. In this sense, a narrative has two kinds of significance or creates two pictures in the mind of the listener: a picture of its subject matter— which is the picture that the speaker *provides*—and a picture of the speaker himself *in action,* saying what he is saying at that moment for his own reasons.[12]

[12]As I. A. Ogden and C. K. Richards put it in their classic work, *The Meaning of Meaning* (New York: Harcourt, Brace and World, 1946), "In speaking a sentence we are giving rise to, as in hearing it we are confronted by, at least two sign-situations" (p. 223). In one of these "sign-situations" the language symbolizes a referent: it denotes something. In the other the statement reflects the speaker in various ways: the nature of his interest, his attitude toward the referent, perhaps his attitude toward the listener, and so forth.

Each kind of significance of an utterance—what it denotes about its referent and what it reflects about the speaker—may be complex. If, for example, a patient says, "I've got to stop eating so much! It's killing me!" the picture of him eating may have various sorts and levels of connotation and metaphorical or symbolic significance. At the same time, the utterance of that statement by him in that particular way and in that particular context may have various kinds of purpose and subjective significance, some perhaps consciously recognized, some not, some essentially communicative, some possibly not.

If it is true in general that an utterance presents us with two pictures, one of its referent and one of the speaker, then, as my example illustrates, the situation of psychotherapy presents us with the special case in which the referent is also as a rule the speaker. In other words, patients very often speak of themselves, or at least of circumstances in which they are central. In this situation, therefore, we are not only confronted by two pictures but, specifically, by two pictures of the patient, one *provided* by him, the other *expressed in his speech act.* One may be a representation of any period of time, the other is necessarily in the present. Each of these pictures might easily (and reasonably) claim the attention and the empathic response of the therapist. Each has a claim of validity, possesses its own intrinsic interest, and (it must be assumed) has some relation to the other. It is the existence of these two pictures and the rivalry between them to which I wish to call attention here; for whether the therapist notices the problem or not, it seems evident that this situation constantly introduces an ambiguity into the application of his principles and techniques. Thus, in regard to the commonplace therapeutic principle of empathy for the patient, one may ask, For which picture of the patient? Or in the proposal that a transference meaning—a significance regarding the patient's attitude toward the therapist—should be found in the patient's feelings, the question is, In which picture of the patient's feelings? Is it in the story that he tells about yesterday's argument with his friend, or in the way that he tells that story to the therapist today?

Often, of course, there is no problem at all; the two pictures are entirely congruent. The patient talks about his feelings with feeling. He says angrily that he feels angry; or he says regretfully that he felt angry then and now regrets it. But it is evident that the two pictures of the patient—one provided by him, the other expressed in his presence—are not necessarily congruent. In particular, it is inherent in the dynamics of the neurotic person that he will often articulate sincerely a picture of himself, of his feelings and thoughts, that is incongruent with the picture the therapist sees and hears before him. The picture he provides is a reflection and a continuation of the dynamics of neurotic self-deception, a distortion, not a communication, of subjective experience.

For example, a young writer begins to speak in his therapy hour, rather abruptly, it seems, immediately on sitting down in the office chair. He says, as if making an announcement, "I hate my father!" He goes on to describe an incident of the day before in which his rather eccentric father had behaved toward him with remarkable and apparently characteristic insensitivity. The patient speaks primarily of his father and his father's behavior, but naturally he is himself a central character in the picture he draws. It is not at all difficult to imagine him in the scene, to imagine his feelings and reactions more or less as he describes them. The therapist has noticed, however, that the patient's initial statement, "I hate my father!" sounded somewhat forced, as if it had been rehearsed; and he says so.

PATIENT *(surprised, perhaps offended, pauses):* Well, I sure hated him yesterday!
THERAPIST: You don't sound so sure about today.
PATIENT: Well . . . I *think* I hate him. . . . *(he pauses again, seems to relax, and proceeds, in a softer voice)* Sometimes I think . . . well, that he's just a loser . . . I feel sorry for him.

It then develops that although the patient actually feels sorry for his father, he thinks that he *should* hate him. The therapist asks why. The patient replies that he thinks he should be "tougher," not so understanding. It is this concern of the patient's, initially unrecognized yet subjectively forceful, that he is not tough enough that prompts him to seize gratefully on an angry feeling when he becomes aware of one and often to persuade himself that he is angrier than he actually is.

Too narrow a view of the therapeutic material, a view limited to what the patient provides, will lead to the therapist's accepting at face value the picture that the patient imagines and constructs of himself as a true picture of his subjective experience when, in fact, it is often a distortion of subjective experience. It can lead to accepting the picture the patient provides as a starting point for the understanding of his dynamics, when in fact the act of drawing that picture should be the starting point. An interpretation of the metaphorical significance of the patient's "hatred" of his father in the case just cited, for example, would be founded on such an error. For the picture that the patient imagines and draws of himself is not a true representation of his subjective experience but is itself a symptomatic self-deception. The actual significance of that picture at the moment lies in the patient's need to construct it.

70

The Words and the Speaker

The Error of Text Analysis

The kind of therapeutic or psychological error that I have just cited is an example of what may be called the error of text analysis. It accepts the narrative text that the patient provides as an expression of his subjective experience when it is actually a consciousness-distorting speech act. Psychoanalysis has, of course, long since accepted in principle Wilhelm Reich's recommendation to pay attention to *how* the patient talks. But there is another, older, contrary psychoanalytic tradition to which psychotherapy in general has also been heir. It is a tradition of text analysis, analysis of the content of associations, subjective reports, or narrative as the expressions and derivatives of mental forces—as the product not so much of a speaker as of a mind. Otto Fenichel puts it as follows: "When the selective conceptual goals of the ego are excluded [by the basic rule], what is expressed is determined rather by tensions and impulses within the individual awaiting the opportunity to gain expression."[13]

But it is not true. This conception of "what is expressed" as, indeed, the conception of free association itself probably derives from the passive associationist psychology of the nineteenth century. We know now that the mind is more actively organized and that behavior, including speech, is more actively directed. No speech of the patient, no matter how earnest his effort to follow the basic rule, can be regarded as mere expression of "tensions and impulses," as a window to the mind, or as mere text. It can be regarded only as language used by a person for purposes recognized or unrecognized—if

[13]Otto Fenichel, *The Psychoanalytic Theory of Neurosis* (New York: W. W. Norton, 1945), p. 24.

71

only for the often unrecognized purpose of being a cooperative patient.

The error of text analysis is not affected by the imaginativeness or even the correctness of the analysis itself—for example, of the metaphorical significance of the text reference. As far as this error is concerned, it does not matter whether, in the case just cited, an actual hatred does exist at some other level or at some other time or in some other context. For the error lies not in asserting the existence of a psychological process that is not, or may not be, present in some form, in some context; it lies rather in overlooking a process that *is* present in this specific context, the dynamic significance of the speech act itself.

The Question of an Observing Ego

I would like to make one further point concerning a premise that is implied in text analysis. Text analysis assumes a neutral or disinterested introspective capacity on the part of the patient, a capacity that enables the patient to stand outside the dynamics of neurosis, including the dynamics of self-deception, and report the mind's experience. This assumption is also contained in the attractive-sounding but problematical concept of "therapeutic alliance," at least in one of its meanings. The supposed "contemplative ego" or "observing ego" of the patient that is critical to such an "alliance" is just such an introspective agency. But the fact that the patient's articulation of his subjective experience serves and is not detached from the dynamics of the neurotic personality precludes reliance on such a "contemplative ego" or any "alliance" that, in turn, depends on it.[14] The same fact casts doubt on the usefulness in general of asking or expecting the patient to "talk about your feelings" or "tell me how that made you feel." For this is precisely what he cannot do in any detached way, without distortion, when those feelings are involved in subjective conflict and neurotic self-deception.[15]

I do not mean to suggest that neurotic individuals are in general incapable of communication that is undistorted by the dynamics of neurosis, or that they are altogether incapable of regarding themselves, or of articulating their own subjective experience, without such distortion. It is only that the picture they have and are able to provide of themselves and their conflict-related subjective experience will inevitably be distorted by the dynamics of self-deception at exactly those points which are at the moment dynamically significant and, therefore, subjectively sensitive. Unaided detachment is not possible at precisely those points at which it would be therapeutically valuable. Even the patient's most cooperative intentions to contribute to the therapeutic effort cannot remove him from the dynamics of his personality.

Here is an example of such an effort, quite similar in its dynamics to the previous case but perhaps more striking. A

[14]Objection to such concepts on these or similar grounds is not new. See Lawrence Friedman's valuable review of the history and various meanings of the concept of therapeutic alliance in his "The Therapeutic Alliance," *International Journal of Psychoanalysis* 50 (1969): 139. This objection would not apply to Freud's view, from which the alliance concept derives, that a nonerotic positive transference strengthens the patient's attachment to therapy and even fosters his "acceptance" of interpretations.

[15]A similar point is made by the author and interviewer Studs Terkel. In the introduction to *Division Street: America* (New York: Pantheon, 1967), speaking of his interviewing method, he says that one gets only clichés from people in response to direct questions about their feelings. It is necessary instead, he says, to talk to them and let them talk to you. And in this case, of course, there is no consideration of any processes of neurotic self-deception.

73

man in his twenties comes in for his therapy hour appearing to be very upset, speaking rather loudly.

PATIENT: It was terrible last night. I've got to learn to control my temper. I really blew up at Doris [his wife]. This can't go on! . . . If it does, she'll leave me! *(As he says this, he gets up and walks around the room. It seems at this point a somewhat exaggerated picture of a distraught man. He continues:)*

All she did was ask me to go out and get something from the store. But I'd had enough. It just got to me, and I yelled and threw things around. . . . It was really something! Why do I do it? *(He then describes further the "terrible" things he did last night, the screaming and shouting, but, again, his description seems somewhat theatrical. He concludes:)* You've got to help me! I can't go on like this! These things really scare her! *(As he finishes, however, a small smile flickers around his mouth.)*

THERAPIST: You seem to have something against smiling.

PATIENT: Well, yeah, I guess I did smile. . . . *(dismissively, now looking sober)* I don't know why.

THERAPIST: Maybe something was funny.

The patient ignores the therapist's remark and starts once again to tell how "terribly angry" he got last night. He adds that, in fact, he is still angry, though he is trying to control himself because he realizes he has "got to stop these blowups." Once again, however, the patient begins, in spite of himself, to smile.

THERAPIST: You still can't make it through the story with a straight face.

The Words and the Speaker

PATIENT *(indignantly):* Are you saying I'm not angry?

THERAPIST: I'm saying that you seem to try not to be amused.

PATIENT *(pauses, momentarily flustered, then seems more relaxed and genuine):* You know, during the fight last night I noticed that I had to turn my head away once or twice. I started to smile then and I had to turn my head away. Why did I do that?

THERAPIST: Perhaps to keep from spoiling the fight.

PATIENT: You mean that was an act last night?

THERAPIST: I suppose, whatever it was, it was like it is today.

PATIENT: Well, it sure scared her.

THERAPIST: Maybe that was the idea.

PATIENT *(laughs):* She always asks me to go to the store at night. . . . *(pauses)* Actually, I don't mind. But that's the thing. I think I'm too easy to push around and she's too bossy.

THERAPIST: "Too easy" to push around, according to what?

PATIENT: I'm weak. I should be like . . . did you see *One Flew over the Cuckoo's Nest?* I should be like MacMurphy, a tiger. She makes me feel declawed.

In the remainder of the hour, it becomes clear that the patient works up the "MacMurphy" act not so much to frighten his wife—at least as an end in itself—as to assure himself that he is not "declawed." (In this respect, the therapist's suggestion that the patient's purpose was to frighten his wife was incorrect.) The patient is quite concerned about being "weak," though he is not initially aware of it. His model of masculine strength is MacMurphy; he thinks that he should be angry like MacMurphy. Perhaps he did feel some anger at his wife when she asked him to go to the store; but it seems likely, if he did, that it was because she inadvertently touched his

75

sensitivity about weakness, not directly because of the nature or even the style of her request. In any case, the articulation in the office of his "anger" is no product of an "observing ego" detached from the dynamics of neurotic conflict. Just the opposite has happened: the "observing ego" has been pressed into the service of the dynamics of self-deception.

These cases suggest a simple generalization concerning the relation between the two pictures of the patient, the one that he articulates (e.g., "terribly angry") and the one he expresses through his presence (e.g., trying not to smile). Whenever there is an incongruence between these two pictures, the picture that the patient articulates will always be the narrower one. The picture the patient provides of his subjective experience encompasses a narrower section of phenomena than the picture of the patient the therapist sees before him. The reason is simple. The view of the patient as he is, the therapist's view, can include an understanding of the picture that the patient provides of himself, not merely as a window to his mind but as an understanding of its use and the subjective necessity for its construction. The picture the patient provides will be an element of the picture the therapist sees, an element of the therapeutic material. Both of these pictures will be available to the therapist's view, while only one is available to the patient. It is surely a critical feature of what we have to offer the patient that our view of him and of what he says is larger than his own.

Chapter 4

_____

The Patient and
the Patient's Problem

In this chapter I will apply and illustrate further the principles and ideas presented in the previous chapter. The selection and arrangement of illustrations is to a large extent arbitrary, since the principles are quite general ones. I have thought it useful, however, to consider various instances of the commonplace therapeutic circumstance in which the patient presents a *problem;* then I have divided these instances into several loose categories. The patient's problem, beginning with the "pre senting problem," probably constitutes the most typical sort of therapeutic content, though it is certainly not the only sort. But there is an additional reason for selecting illustrations of this kind. Some problems presented by the patient—especially those presented with great urgency—can command the therapist's attention in a way that is actually disadvantageous to the therapeutic work. That work, after all, is not to help the patient solve his problem, but to help *him* so that *he* can solve his problem.

The "Presenting Problem" and the Patient's Expectations

People come to therapy in distress, with problems in mind that they have identified as the source of their distress, and that they have at least tentatively concluded they cannot solve by themselves. Sometimes these problems are classical psychiatric symptoms; usually they are not. These people come for help; they want their distress relieved. But it is in the nature of neurotic distress that the patient cannot have a clear idea of its true cause and may not even have a clear sense of its actual quality. The patient's notion of the nature of his distress and therefore of the form that relief may take is bound to be affected by the neurotic process itself. In short, the "presenting problem" will appear to the patient, and be described by him, according to ideas and concerns about himself that are not themselves independent of the neurotic process and may even be products of it.

Consider, for example, the depressed woman cited in chapter 2 who has been persuaded by her husband, or by his reactions to her, that she is an "uninteresting," sexually inadequate, and "inhibited" person. She describes herself and her "problem" in those terms in the initial hour. The words she uses to describe herself and her various insufficiencies have originated with her husband and carry his authority, which is, as far as she is concerned, hardly distinguishable from truth.

This patient comes to therapy in the same spirit, or in the

The Patient and the Patient's Problem

same dispirited way, as she has previously tried to study news magazines and to take various classes in order to make herself "more interesting." These efforts having failed—that is, having failed to satisfy her husband—she tries another perhaps more authoritative route to self-improvement, as she sees it. In describing her problem, she may even speak of her need for greater "self-confidence." But she imagines that change too, though she does not realize it, only as it may make her more satisfactory in her husband's eyes. She does not imagine that greater self-confidence may have the result that her husband's criticisms will carry less weight, or that she will reject them altogether.

The idea is sometimes proposed of a "therapeutic contract" between patient and therapist, an agreement regarding the aims of therapy. But as the case just mentioned illustrates, the fact that the nature of the patient's expectations of therapeutic help, as well as his idea of the nature of his problem, will be affected by the neurotic condition itself makes it clear that the idea of such a contract is not sound. A contract, after all, assumes that both parties share a clear understanding of the meaning and implications of its terms, and in this case one party is not in a position to have such an understanding.

Along with presenting his problem, the patient quite often volunteers additional information about himself. The presentation of such information, even the selection of biographical information offered, likewise cannot be assumed to be independent of the subjective dynamics of the neurotic process.

A lawyer, at the first meeting with the therapist, describes his phobia—he cannot drive on freeways—with considerable embarrassment. He somewhat nervously anticipates biographical questions ("You're probably interested in my childhood"). He seems to anticipate certain rather specific biographical questions, and he volunteers—bravely, it seems, as if admitting something difficult—that he was the youngest of three children and was "probably overprotected" by his mother.

The significance of this admission, it turns out, derives from his conviction that his mother, in this way, made him a "sissy." He vaguely relates the existence of his present fearfulness and indeed the present necessity for therapy to this fault of his upbringing. His present troubles seem to him a reflection of the lifelong weakness of character of which he already felt ashamed, and which he now seems determined to face and overcome. He concludes the story, or admission, of what he considers to be the central circumstance of his childhood by looking at the therapist and saying, "Go ahead, shoot!" as though braced for the worst.

The fact that the "presenting problem," as the patient sees it and is able to formulate it, is not independent of the dynamics of the neurotic personality does not diminish its significance or in itself discredit its facts. It simply means that that problem and those facts can be fully understood only in their immediate context as his presentation, the product of his point of view or of his subjective requirements. That point of view and those requirements may not be simple, are probably not recognized by the patient himself, and may themselves be symptomatic.

For example, a woman in her early thirties, an architect, describes in her first hour the problem that brings her to therapy, with a brisk, somewhat tense directness. She says that she often has about her a "challenging" and "harsh" quality that she is unable to control and that "turns people off." She cites several examples, but it is clear that she is particularly concerned that she "can't keep a boyfriend." She is afraid, she says, that she will spend her life lonely and unmarried and, as she says this, her briskness fades and she looks quite depressed.

The Patient and the Patient's Problem

She adds finally: "The harshness even turns me off." She wants, she says, to be "more soft and feminine." It is clear that this is the goal she hopes to achieve in psychotherapy.

As one listens to this woman's problem and sees her, two things become clear. First, it is easy to imagine that her rather forced and tense directness may, at times, be sharpened to the point of seeming "challenging" and "harsh." Second, it is plain that she regards herself with extreme and essentially unrecognized prejudice. In other words, the "problem" she describes may be real enough; for that matter, so may be its social consequences. But her view of this problem, even her identification of it, is greatly prejudiced by a larger neurotic problem, her sense of personal inadequacy, of not being what she thinks she should be ("soft and feminine"). And this problem is essentially invisible to her. Thus, she sees her social problem, as well as her distaste for herself, only as reasonable reactions to her actual personal deficiencies. The therapist, by contrast, is in a position to see her distaste for herself and her sense of inadequacy as more fundamental than that; in fact, he can see in these an attitude toward herself that probably existed prior to her "harshness" and may underly it. She thinks of her "harshness" as being responsible for her distaste for herself. But he sees that the situation can be better understood the other way around: her unrecognized sense of inadequacy and distaste for herself may be responsible for a quality of defensiveness ("harshness"). Her attitude affects her therapeutic expectations. As she sees the therapeutic prospect, if she were made into something closer to what she should be ("soft and feminine"), she would be more attractive to men and would no longer "turn [herself] off." From the therapist's standpoint, the quality of that concern reflects the attitude of one who is more profoundly "turned off" by herself than she realizes. From his standpoint, if she could be relieved of her long-familiar sense of her own inadequacy, she would be less concerned with conforming to that model, would probably be less defensive, and would certainly enjoy life more.

A viewpoint of this sort on the therapist's part, in regard to the "presenting problem," may be greeted by a patient with a particular kind of ambivalence. On the one hand, this viewpoint throws a new and unexpected light on that problem, and this is a relief. On the other hand, for the therapist to articulate and thus to bring into question the unrecognized attitudes and prejudices that have surrounded, colored, and even defined what the patient has considered his chief "problem" may prompt concern that the problem itself is being slighted. The patient begins to realize that the therapist's interest is not exactly where he expected it to be; it is not directed solely at the "problem" but includes unexpected aspects of the patient. He may become concerned, for example, that the therapist's aim is that he "accept himself"; that is, resign himself to what he has considered to be his problem and give up hope for its change. It should be clear, to the therapist at least, that that is not the point. When the therapist suggests that the patient's attitude toward his symptom is itself symptomatic, his point is not to diminish the importance of the "presenting" symptom but to enlarge its context. It is not to deny the reality of the problem that has been presented, but to show that it is part of a larger "problem," in the form of the patient himself.

The Patient and the Patient's Problem

Two Views of the Problem

My examples have already reflected the fact that the patient's view of his problem and the therapist's view of the patient's problem will be different. I would like to illustrate that difference of views still more sharply. The patient sees the problem according to his perspective, but he cannot see the perspective itself. The therapist is in a position to see both. The patient points to a problem. The therapist cannot ignore that problem to which the patient points, but he has a wider view of it, which includes the patient pointing as well.

For example, a thirty-one-year-old woman who has been seen in psychotherapy for about six months comes this day with a special problem. She is a timid person, much concerned with others' expectations and her own inadequacies. She is also a dutiful person, concerned with what she should be doing and feeling and, in general, with what she should be like. She was quite depressed when she came to therapy initially, and her idea in coming was that it might help her become the sort of person—more open, spontaneous, self-confident—she thought she should be. Recently she has been less depressed and, for the first time since her marriage, has taken a job. It is this job that has raised the problem that concerns her today.

She likes the job very much and had been quite pleased with herself as well, but she has learned now that she is underpaid. She feels, therefore, that she should ask for a raise. But, she says, she is afraid to do so. She observes that the reasons she has offered herself for hesitating are mere rationalizations: it is a small office and business is not very good, she is no prize as a secretary, and so forth. But, she says, she realizes that the essential reason for not having asked is her timidity. The problem has become especially distressing now because her husband and friends have been urging her to be more "assertive" and to ask for the raise. Money is not the issue, but they feel it would be good for her—good for her self-confidence, particularly—to ask. She says that she herself feels it "would be the healthy" thing to do, but it is terribly difficult.

She turns to the therapist with the question, "What do you think? It would be the healthy thing to do, wouldn't it?" She puts the question as if already all but resigned to the answer and to her fate.

The neurotic problem that the patient sees and points to is clear: she is intimidated by her boss. At the moment, however, though she does not realize it, the problem of intimidation by her boss is not the only problem, nor even the most pressing one, she experiences. For it is not the weight of the boss's authority and expectations that is most intimidating now, but rather the expectations of her husband and family, which are given special weight for her by the requirements of mental health (as she understands them). Her responsibility to satisfy these expectations and requirements (to do what is "good for her") clearly outweighs in its authority the ordeal of going to her boss. She is ready to face him, but she does not dare to oppose them. Only the therapist's authority on matters of mental health might offer a reprieve.

This oppressive sense of obligation to do the "healthy" thing is the more immediate expression of the neurotic problem. It is at the moment the focus of the subjective dynamics of her personality, and she visibly experiences its subjective effects. Yet it is invisible to her. The direction of her attention is determined by the pressure of this intimidating responsibility; but the fact that she is intimidated by it, along with the simple fact that her own comfort commands no respect at all from her, she cannot see. She cannot see the present form of the problem precisely because of the subjective force with which she experiences it; she cannot recognize the present form of intimidating authority precisely because it directs her attention elsewhere. It is for the therapist to show her *this* problem and the view it offers of the problem she presents. The point is not to brush aside the problem she presents in favor of the more immediate one. It is to make it possible for her to resolve the problem she presents by affecting her perspective on it.

It is interesting, also, to consider the meaning of "assertiveness" from these two views. From the patient's perspective, a "healthy" assertiveness would consist of facing her employer and asking for a raise. But from the larger view—the view that encompasses the patient herself—the very action that seems assertive to the patient is, in the present context, only dutiful and obedient. If assertiveness means the freedom to recognize and respect one's own wishes, then for this woman at this time it would surely mean refusing to subject herself to such an ordeal.

In a certain sense, however, apart from context, both views are correct. She is intimidated both by her employer *and* by the authoritative rules of mental health, as she imagines them. Both are symptomatic of the same neurotic personality, and the symptoms are fairly similar in form. These facts have an interesting therapeutic implication. They imply that any therapeutic contribution toward freeing the patient from the more immediate intimidation by her friends' and husband's expectations and the authority of "mental health" will also contribute to freeing her from intimidation by the authoritative figure of her boss. If the patient comes to feel freer to refuse to ask for a raise now, when to do so would merely satisfy external rules and expectations, she will feel freer to ask for a raise in the future when she wishes to.

On the other hand, it seems evident that the therapist who

becomes absorbed in the problem as it is originally articulated by the patient, addressing himself only to her deference to her employer, makes a mistake of two kinds. First, he fails to recognize the presence of the neurotic conflict where it is now experienced. Second—and perhaps more important—if the therapist accepts the patient's own perspective, in effect he confirms and adds his weight to its premises. The therapist then tacitly accepts, as the patient does, the necessity for the patient to satisfy these external rules and expectations and to subordinate her own wishes or judgment to them. If he does that, the therapist may contribute to the patient's achievement of a behavioral simulation of assertiveness and mental health but will not actually have advanced her self-respect or self-confidence. This hypothetical possibility may remind us that therapists, too, have only a limited view of their own activity and may, in their absorption in what they are saying, lose sight of the fact that for them, too, saying something is doing something.

Two Representations of the Same Problem

Sometimes it happens that the patient points to a problem of his, perhaps a symptomatic attitude or reaction, with absolute accuracy, yet does so with an attitude that repeats in the office the very problem to which he is pointing. He describes the problem, on the one hand; and he lives it, on the other. Thus the therapist witnesses two representations of the same problem, while the patient can see only one. The case just cited is, to a certain extent, an example of this circumstance. A still more clear example follows.

The Patient and the Patient's Problem

A tense, quite driven businessman in his early thirties comes to his therapy hour in an agitated state. He begins to talk at once: "What's the matter with me! I was just looking for a parking space and I spotted one and some guy cut in front of me. You know me! I had to pull up alongside of him and give him a blast and let him know what I thought of him! I couldn't let it go! I can't let anything go! The wear and tear I cause myself! I can't take anything in stride!"

The patient describes himself accurately in this diatribe. At the same time, it is a diatribe. The attitude and the emotional state he describes in himself as he was ten minutes before on the street are much the same as those he expresses in the office now. Neither any offense against him nor any failing of his own can be taken "in stride." As he says, he "can't let anything go." He must do something about each such wrong, take action, punish, not let the perpetrator get away with it. For present purposes, we do not need to understand much further the subjective dynamics associated with this general attitude; let us imagine, simply, that to do otherwise would be from his standpoint weak, passive, irresponsible, or complacent.

If it is true that the patient's attitude and the dynamics of the episode on the street are closely similar to those of his diatribe in the office, then the question may be raised once again whether one would not come to the same understanding, the same result, whichever was addressed by the therapist. Why not then simply address the patient's problem as it is presented by him, in the form of his reaction on the street, an episode in which he certainly appears to be already interested?

But the fact is that he is, at the moment, not merely interested in his earlier reaction. He is interested in punishing himself for what he considers a failing, as a schoolboy might be punished for failing to learn a lesson. His contemptuous description of the episode serves that aim. There is no reason for the therapist to deny the reality of his earlier reaction, but to speak only of it while ignoring the present reaction is tacitly to join his cause and to offer further material for his contempt. There is also, as before, a second reason to give attention to his present reaction. While it may be true that the same attitudes are contained in both the earlier reaction and the present one, it is the present one that he is living. It is the present reaction that drives him, and the present reaction whose effects he experiences. To join him in his present interest is indeed what the patient expects, and he would probably be satisfied by it. But to articulate the nature of that interest will relieve him in a way that he did not expect and will contribute to his change.

Problems of Special Urgency

A problem that is presented with great urgency commands attention. When a patient presents a problem in that way ("You've got to help me!"), the therapist may find it difficult to resist giving his own attention entirely to the problem that is the object of such urgency, sometimes overlooking the patient as he sits and speaks before him. The therapist in that case reacts to the patient's urgency with such completeness that he is in no better position than the patient to consider it. For the urgency itself is as much the therapeutic material as the problem that is its object. Sometimes—especially in the case of driven, compulsive individuals—the urgency with which a problem is presented expresses the unrecognized imperative attitude of the patient toward himself in regard to the matter at hand.

The Patient and the Patient's Problem

For example: A woman in her early fifties had, since the death of her close woman friend and companion some five months before, become increasingly depressed, instead of recovering as she and her family had expected of her. Recently, in fact, she had begun to drink heavily, arousing both their concern and her own. She appeared in the first hour to be quite tense and agitated, even angry with herself, as she described the events that had brought her to a therapist.

> PATIENT: It's been five months! I have to start putting my life together, start working again! But instead of getting better, I'm getting worse! And now I've started to drink! ... *(She continues in this vein, with repeated references to the calendar.)*
>
> THERAPIST: *(interrupting):* You seem to be an impatient person.
>
> PATIENT: Impatient? But it's been five months!
>
> THERAPIST: Yes, I understand that. But you seem very conscious of some sort of schedule you must meet, and that I don't understand.

The patient becomes quiet and starts to cry. She then proceeds to describe her determination, starting almost immediately after her friend's death and continuing ever since, apparently more or less relentlessly, to "get hold of" herself, to rearrange her living situation according to a family plan, and to go to work. But, she adds, she has not been sure where she wants to live, or that she likes the tentative plans that her family had made for her. When she says that she has not been sure that she likes those plans, it seems clear that she is quite sure that she does not like them.

Obsessive-compulsive patients often present their dilemmas

and problems of decision with great urgency. They feel they must *decide* or *do something.* These people frequently mean, by deciding or doing something, doing something that they do not want to do but think they should. They often have an unrecognized prejudice in favor of the decision that represents change, the one that is more difficult and that feels, for those reasons, more active and decisive. Consequently, they do not regard a decision to continue as before as a decision or as doing something at all. The urgency and agony of decision are often intensified for them by an acute awareness of the necessity to decide or to do something by a certain deadline. Sometimes such deadlines are self-imposed and objectively rather arbitrary, being simply devices by which the compulsive person intensifies the pressure on himself to do what he thinks he should. Sometimes, however, the awareness of an objective deadline (such as a "last chance" to do something) will trigger a great intensification of such pressure, full of agonizing soul-searching.

In these cases, the urgency with which the "problem"—or the necessity to reach a decision—is presented will often not only be aimed at the patient himself ("I've got to make a decision now!") but will also include the therapist ("I hope you're not one of those passive therapists!"). The patient, under great pressure himself, hopes to find relief in the form of an authoritative answer to the problem of what "should" be done. It may easily happen that the therapist, responding to the patient's urgent presentation, will join the patient in sifting through the pros and cons of alternatives, hoping to find a solution. But he will soon realize that no solution is to be found that way. The patient's obsessive conscientiousness requires him to search for, and find, arguments against any solution, especially one that at first looks attractive.

90

The Patient and the Patient's Problem

One such patient, who had been relatively comfortably separated from her husband, is thrown into agonizing indecision by his "final offer" to resume their unsatisfactory marriage. She rejects divorce as "a lonely life that I wouldn't want"; at the same time, returning is a senseless "postponing of the inevitable." She turns to the therapist: "I've got to make a decision now!"

It is easy enough for the therapist to become exasperated at such times if he feels pressed by the patient's urgency. He may even be inclined to reproach the patient for attempting to "shift the responsibility for the decision" to him. That understanding may actually be correct enough, but it fails to consider that for such a person the experience of deciding has become so tortured as to drive anyone to seek relief.

It is for the therapist to see, as the patient cannot, that the problem cannot be solved as the patient presents it. It is for the therapist to recognize the prejudice in the patient's picture of the problem that the patient herself cannot recognize. That prejudice is contained in the quality of the urgency itself, in the attitude of "I must do something now!" (which means, "I must do something different from what I am already doing" or "I must do what I don't want to do" or, at the very least, "I must very seriously consider every argument in favor of doing what I don't want to do"). The meaning and aim of that urgency must be articulated, for only the relief of that urgency can recast the "problem" in more soluble terms. Relief of that urgency and pressure exerted by the patient on herself will permit the patient to achieve some clearer sense of what she wants to do.

Another example: A professional woman in her late thirties, married and with a fourteen-year-old child, is in a state of agitation because of her unplanned pregnancy. The problem is, she says, that although she had often considered a second child, she had always "put it off." Now, she says with urgency, she does not know what she wants to do, what she "really" wants to do, and she has been agonizing over it for weeks. Furthermore, there are not one but two deadlines. The deadline for an abortion is approaching, and the age limit for bearing children is also coming close. She says she "must decide! And soon!" If she wants to have another baby, now is the time to have it! When she thinks of having an abortion, she says, it makes her feel sad. Besides, she adds, looking urgently at the therapist, another child would be company in her old age!

THERAPIST: But *I* have nothing against your having a baby.
PATIENT *(somewhat flustered):* Well . . . it's just that my work. . . . *(She explains that her career, at which she has worked very hard, is just approaching real success and a baby would definitely interrupt it. Specifically, pregnancy and a baby would put an end to the important and interesting project in which she is now engaged.)* But *(emphatically, with a somewhat forced emotion)* when I saw Mary [a friend] and her baby together, their closeness, it looked wonderful. . . . It almost makes me feel like going ahead.
THERAPIST: "Almost"?
PATIENT *(again momentarily flustered, then exclaiming):* Why don't I want another baby? Any normal woman would! It's not normal!

The conscious articulation of the patient's feelings, of the conflict between what she thinks she should want ("Any normal woman would!") and what she actually does want, is not necessarily concluded at this point, but it is underway. The enlargement of the patient's self-awareness ("Why don't I

want another baby!") was initiated by the therapist's recognition (" 'Almost'?") of her effort to find within herself a desire
that she thought she should have and thought she might have
but did not find. It was this prejudiced and unrecognized effort
of hers, made urgent by a "last chance," that created the
problem of decision in its original and insoluble form.

Is the Patient's Story True?

It sometimes happens that the story the patient tells or the
problem he relates seems to the therapist implausible and difficult to believe. Therapists often are disconcerted by this
doubt. A dilemma is created for them. They do not like to
pretend acceptance of the story as fact, but they are reluctant
to express their skepticism and, as it usually seems, to antago-
nize the patient. The latter course is made additionally difficult
by the therapist's realization that he has no independent access
to the facts and thus is in no strong position to dispute them.

For example, a therapist describes such a dilemma in connection with a patient who regularly "makes a case" that she
was the victim of unfair treatment as a child. It seems that the
patient insists that her siblings were given preferred treatment
in ways and to an extent that the therapist, an experienced
person, finds hard to believe and thinks must be exaggerated.
At the same time, the therapist says that he recognizes that
these stories "just might" be true. Therefore, he says, he does
not know how to respond.

The therapist here misses the point; he is not looking in the
right direction. For the matter of therapeutic interest—the
therapeutic material—is not fundamentally the relation of the

patient's story to reality, but the patient's relation to her story. It is not only the story but also the significance of the story for the patient, including her aim in telling it, what she is *doing* by telling it in the way that she tells it, that is important. In this instance, it is the very fact, noticed by the therapist but not seriously considered, that the patient "makes a case"—in other words, tries to persuade one or both of them of the reality of her grievance—that is the relevant matter. It is this unrecognized self-deceptive effort that, at the moment, separates the patient from an awareness of her actual feelings and convictions.

My point is not at all the same as the view that holds that such a story is, in any case, "true for the patient." On the contrary, if the therapist has a sense of a story's implausibility, and especially if he recognizes that the patient is "making a case" for it, it is most likely because it is *not* true for the patient, though the patient tries to believe that it is. If the patient tells even a remarkable story with genuine conviction, the therapist will probably find it believable or, at worst, a naïve and unprejudiced mistake.

Chapter 5

Reactions to
the Therapist

This chapter considers the special category of therapeutic material that consists of the patient's attitudes and reactions to the therapist. Essentially this category comprises the clinical phenomena usually described as transference, though I will refer to certain additional issues of the patient's relationship with the therapist as well. The term transference, of course, not only refers to clinical phenomena but also implies a specific theoretical understanding of them in terms of personal history. The clinical phenomena are well established, but the theoretical understanding is, in my opinion, quite arguable. (I argue against that theoretical understanding in chapter 8.) In any case, two levels or kinds of transference interpretation have been distinguished in psychoanalysis: the articulation of a reaction or attitude toward the therapist; and the interpretation of the presumed historical prototype of that reaction or attitude.

It is the first, whose therapeutic value is undisputed, that will concern us here.[1]

How Unique Is "Transference Material"?

Transference has occupied a central and unique place in the theory of psychoanalytic therapy and, if anything, that position has received even greater emphasis recently.[2] The reason for this emphasis seems clear: transference has been thought to reproduce, in the patient's attitude and feelings toward the therapist, the dynamics of the neurosis within the therapeutic office. In psychoanalysis, that re-creation has also meant that transference affords a unique opportunity to reconstruct the basis of those dynamics in childhood history and fantasy and to interpret them in an especially immediate and concrete way. Even apart from that further step of reconstruction, however, it is clear that transference has represented for psychoanalysis a unique kind of therapeutic material. It has represented a unique opportunity to confront the workings of the neurosis in the "here and now." In Freud's well-known figure of speech, "no one can be slain *in absentia.*"[3]

From our standpoint, it must be said that the phenomenon of transference loses some, though not all, of its uniqueness as therapeutic material. It has acquired that uniqueness, after all, from the contrast between its immediacy and the comparative

[1]See Merton M. Gill, *Analysis of Transference*, Psychological Issues 353 (New York: International Universities Press, 1982), vol. I. Gill's therapeutic emphasis is clearly on the first type of interpretation.

[2]See Gill, *Analysis of Transference* [1], vol. I.

[3]Sigmund Freud, "The Dynamics of Transference" (1912), *Standard Edition*, 12:108 (London: Hogarth Press, 1958).

emotional distance of the more general narrative content. The contrast is between therapeutic material that is lived in the office and therapeutic material that consists of what is talked about in the office (*"in absentia"*) but has been lived elsewhere. In the traditional psychoanalytic context, transference constitutes one of two kinds of reaction—resistance is the other— that more or less compels the therapist to turn his attention from the content of what the patient provides to the presence of the patient. These reactions command a different attention from the therapist simply because, in one way or another, they interrupt the narrative content. In the case of the transference reaction, if the narrative is not actually interrupted, the narrative content itself may call attention to the fact that the telling of it constitutes a present *reaction;* and in that sense it interrupts itself. It is in this that the uniqueness of transference lies: it is a present reaction, not a story about a reaction, and it commands the therapist's attention sharply to the present and to the person before him. But from the standpoint proposed here, the patient and the patient's reaction are *continuously* the focus of the therapist's attention. The dynamics of the neurotic personality is recognized continuously within the office, not only in the patient's reaction to the therapist but, whatever the patient's interest, in the activity of saying or doing what he does in the way that he does.

Viewed from this standpoint, transference loses its distinctiveness as therapeutic material in a further sense. When every statement made by the patient is recognized as a speech act and not merely followed as text, then in a certain sense the relationship with the therapist is continuously, not just sporadically, an aspect of the therapeutic material. The therapist is only sporadically the subject of the patient's narrative interest; but he is continuously the object of the patient's communication. Every distortion of the communicative aim of speech, every use of speech for another, unrecognized purpose is from this standpoint a distortion or an impairment of the patient's communicative relationship with the therapist. Every neurotic self-deception implies an impairment of that relationship. It cannot be otherwise. When the neurotic person is estranged from his actual feelings and in the very process of deceiving himself, he cannot at the same time communicate genuinely with the therapist. In Kaiser's phrase, the patient "doesn't talk straight."

For example, when the patient enters the room saying loudly and somewhat theatrically, in self-reproach, "I've got to stop eating so much! It's killing me!" he is not, at that moment, talking *to* the therapist. Similarly, when another patient says "I hate my father!" as if he had been rehearsing the speech, he is not simply communicating his feelings to the therapist. On the contrary, the unrecognized aim of his utterance is to feel something that he does not at that moment actually feel.

This kind of impairment of the communicative relationship cannot properly be described as a transference reaction. It is a more general phenomenon, an inevitable extension of the patient's self-estrangement. Indeed, very often to articulate the unrecognized distortion of communication—how something is said—is to articulate, in the same stroke, the process of self-deception.

The Therapist as the Subject of Conflict

Inevitably, the therapist himself becomes not only the object of the patient's communication but also a subject of neurotic conflict and concern. It is that development which contains the clinical phenenomena familiar as transference. To one degree or another, the relationship with the therapist becomes the immediate occasion of characteristic forms of internal conflict and anxiety and of the restrictive and corrective reactions, distortions of self-awareness, and inhibitions of behavior required to avoid or dispel that conflict and anxiety.

It was Freud's idea that a certain psychological correspondence, even a kind of psychological equivalence, exists between the symptom neurosis on the one hand and the transference on the other. This equivalence is expressed in his conception that the fantasies and anxieties of the infantile conflict, represented in the adult patient's symptom neurosis, are transferred under the special condition of the analytic situation to the patient's relationship with the analyst. Thus the symptom neurosis is transformed into a "transference neurosis." I will argue against the conception of such a transfer; but one thing is indisputable. The dynamics of the neurotic personality are brought into the office and are engaged by the relationship with the therapist. How could it not be so? A way of being, after all, is also a way of relating. The therapist, if the treatment is effective at all, comes to be a significant figure in the patient's life. It is inevitable that this relationship, as well as the patient's reaction to the therapeutic situation itself, should engage the characteristic dynamics of his personality.

It is important to make clear the nature of the therapeutic interest in the patient's reactions and attitudes toward the therapist. The point of this interest is not merely to identify, in what the patient says, the existence or the source of a fantasy, a wish, an "inappropriate" feeling, or any other mental content. The point is not, as it might have been for the isolated symptom neurosis, to identify in this way a nuclear conflict within the patient. The point is to articulate *the workings of a personality* as it is expressed in the relationship in which the patient is at the moment engaged. The relationship with the therapist has triggered and engaged the subjective dynamics of the patient's personality much as any other important relationship might. It has done so not so much because of the therapist's personality as on account of the relationship created by the therapeutic situation. That relationship has triggered reactions in the patient, prompted restrictive and corrective reactions of the personality against itself, and led to distortions of self-awareness and anxiety-forestalling restrictions and distortions of the relationship itself. In this connection, we may paraphrase Kaiser's observation that the patient does not "talk straight" to a broader observation that the patient cannot relate straight—that is, cannot "be himself" in this relationship. The consciousness-distorting dynamics of the neurotic personality that prevent him from being "fully behind" what he says also prevent him from knowing what he feels, or sometimes from realizing that he has any feelings at all, in regard to the therapist.[4]

For example, a young businessman, who has repeatedly had difficult relationships with various bosses, talks to the therapist with a kind of forced breeziness or exaggerated casualness. He seems to make an effort, in this way, to speak to the therapist as though to an equal. He addresses the therapist, some years older, by a familiar nickname. Sometimes he is concerned and insistent that arrangements and privileges, such as cancellation privileges, be equal between him and the therapist.

Thus it appears that a concern with status—a concern that is probably characteristic—is activated or intensified by the therapeutic relationship. It is a concern and a sensitivity of someone who feels inferior to the other one, of someone who respects the other more than he respects himself, but does not

[4]See Gill, *Analysis of Transference* [1], vol. I.

know it. He does not know it because he is prompted by the very sensation of that inferiority or shame to simulate self-confidence. The relation of equality and familiarity with the therapist that he attempts to sustain is based on that self-deception.

The therapist begins to articulate that subjective world:

> THERAPIST: You seem anxious to show me that I am no more important than you.
> PATIENT *(angrily, no longer breezy):* You're not!

As this case illustrates, a patient's reaction to the therapeutic relationship depends not only on the individual dynamics of the patient's personality but also on the special conditions of the relationship itself. Obviously these conditions vary with the therapeutic method, the personality of the therapist, and so forth, but certain ones are general. The patient comes for help, the therapist to help; the patient pays, the therapist is paid; the therapist is responsible for the arrangements in a general way, while the patient, if he stays, is expected to accept them. Freud noted that the analytic situation did, in fact, have some resemblance to the child's relation to the parent.[5] It seems to be true, at least, that most—possibly all—patients have an exaggerated notion of the therapist's authority. If this is so, perhaps it is also a reflection of the neurotic person's generally diminished sense of himself and of his own authority, a reflection of his own sense of being less than a qualified grownup. At any rate, such a sensation is common among patients, and it is evident in a variety of reactions of different kinds of personality to the therapeutic relationship.

Some patients, like the person just cited, resent the relation-

[5]Freud, "Dynamics of Transference" [3], p. 100.

ship from the beginning as an intrinsic indignity. They are painfully conscious, as this patient was, of any distinction in role and endow it with the significance of distinction in rank. They feel diminished, without being aware of it, in the presence of someone they suppose to be of high rank, and they become more defensive of their dignity. Other patients, more conscious of what they consider their inadequacies, "keep their place" as patients, perhaps with an exaggerated deference and often by severely restricting the nature of their communication. They experience an oppressive, though probably sporadic, concern with being satisfactory to the therapist, with being "interesting enough" or in some other way "a good patient." These concerns, unrecognized by the patients themselves, are often peripheral as long as the patient is occupied with matters external to the therapeutic relationship and as long as the patient feels that he is satisfying the requirements of his role. But the concerns are activated as soon as the patient is tempted to stray outside that essentially humble self-defined role or to forget his "place," or often when the patient is for one reason or another momentarily at a loss to fulfill that role. Frequently, this occurs when the patient feels relatively better and, therefore, has "nothing to say," that is, nothing that feels sufficiently patientlike. One patient expressed the view that it would be "insolent" to talk about anything to the therapist except "you know, pressing problems." The activation of such concerns is likely to trigger, in turn, anxiety-dispelling corrective action in the form, for instance, of renewed offerings of such "problems."

A somewhat different sort of self-imposed restriction is a reflection less of attitudes or conflict directly concerned with the therapist than of more general attitudes of the patient toward himself. For example, certain patients are quite conscious of a responsibility to avoid "wasting time." In one such instance, a patient, just returned from a trip, begins to tell about it with enthusiasm, then abruptly stops himself. The therapist remarks on the abruptness with which he stops. The patient says, rather severely, "That's not what I'm here for!"

But it is evident that such dutiful restrictions, consciously intended to promote work, also contain implicit prohibitions regarding the relationship with the therapist. That is, the attitude "Stick to business!" implies a prohibition against any departure from businesslike and consciously purposeful communication with the therapist or any personal interest in him. In such a case, the continuity of anxiety-forestalling restrictions and distortions of the relationship with more general restrictive and consciousness-distorting attitudes is especially clear.

In general, the patient himself is quite unaware of the nature of such restrictive attitudes or of their existence, or even of the self-imposed limitations of communication they require.

For example, a patient, feeling somewhat better that day, declares that his mind is "a blank—nothing at all to say." (He does not count that remark as saying something.) The therapist replies that the condition of a "blank" mind seems unlikely, to which the patient replies, "No, really. Absolutely nothing . . . that would be helpful." It should be remembered that such apparently small unrecognized restrictions of communication actually reflect similarly unrecognized conflict-forestalling restrictions and distortions of the general form of the therapeutic relationship. In obsessive-compulsive patients, particularly, they often reflect the patient's unnoticed consciousness of his patient-ness and careful direction of himself according to his proper "role," as he imagines it. The various requirements, prohibitions, and anxieties implied in the patient's conception of his "role"—indeed, the adherence to such a "role" in the communicative relationship—may easily be overlooked by the therapist until some particular circumstance brings them to light.

For example, a male teacher in his thirties seemed to talk in a quiet, methodical, but not dry way. His attitude toward the therapist was friendly and, if it contained reserve, it was not of a conspicuous kind—not until the following exchange, at least.

PATIENT: I'm tired. . . . *(explains that he worked late the previous night)* I can't think of anything to say, anything to discuss.

THERAPIST: Maybe you think you must limit yourself here to "discussing," that is, to concentrating on a problem. You don't let yourself simply talk.

PATIENT: Well . . . it's like when I go to my doctor or my dentist. I don't hold anything back. I'd tell you everything *you needed to know* [my emphasis]. I wouldn't hold anything back knowingly, even if it were embarrassing. But, I mean, I wouldn't talk about music.

THERAPIST: Oh?

PATIENT: Well, yeah. Look, I wouldn't use foul language either. You're my therapist!

THERAPIST: Yes, I am, but I don't see why it follows that you must talk to me only in a certain way.

PATIENT: Look, when I was in school, we had an orchestra and we'd go to different schools and places to give concerts, and the music teacher, who was the conductor, would be with us. We had a good time. He was a nice guy and we knew him pretty well. But I was always reserved, more than the others. Even though he was "one of the boys," I knew he was a teacher. There was a gap between us.

THERAPIST: Yes, of course there was a gap, but it sounds like you were very conscious of that gap and very careful to respect it.

These examples illustrate a further point, concerning the difference that I discussed in the previous chapter between the problem that the patient sees and brings to the therapy and the larger context in which the therapist is able to see that problem, including its relation to the patient himself. As I have said, the patient is often unaware even that he *has* an attitude toward the therapist, let alone a restrictive or conflictual one. But as these examples show, sooner or later that unrecognized attitude is likely to create a problem for the patient in relation to the therapist, such as the problem here of being temporarily at a loss to provide him with satisfactory "material." The patient will then experience a problem in the therapeutic situation but will not be in a position to see that it is his perspective that creates it, at least in the form that it has for him. To see that, he needs the therapist's help.

For example, a rather timid young woman has been silent for a few moments in her therapy hour and looks somewhat uncomfortable. The therapist has made some remark to that effect.

PATIENT *(responding, apologetically):* I can't think of any thing to say.
THERAPIST: I must seem impatient.
PATIENT: No. But I know you're waiting. I know you must be expecting me to say something.
THERAPIST: Yes, I suppose I am; you usually do. But you seem to feel that you have the responsibility to satisfy my expectation.

It is worth noting that here, as in general, the patient's relation to the problem that she sees (not having "anything to say") is expressed in the way she presents that problem, apologetically.

The Expression of the Therapeutic Relationship

The patient's reactions and attitudes to the therapist and the therapeutic situation are probably in most ways not essentially different from his reactions to other comparable figures and circumstances that he might talk about in the therapy hour. But it is obvious that, as far as the communication in the hour of those reactions to the therapist is concerned, there is a critical difference: the one who is talked *about* is also the one who is talked *to*. This situation is bound to affect the meaning of anything said about him or in any way referring to him. Any statement referring to the therapist is not only a speech act in the sense that any other utterance is. It becomes in this situation an action conscious of itself in a special way, an action whose purpose must be presumed to include the effect of its utterance on the therapist. The *act* of saying anything about the therapist, in his presence, becomes self-evidently an additional communication to him. The additional communication consists of the significance of the fact, known to both, that his patient is saying this about him. In this way, for example, a concern about the effectiveness of the therapy, when expressed to the therapist, becomes a complaint. A report to the therapist of a sexual fantasy about him becomes an erotic act. Thus, a twenty-four-year-old divorced female patient tells her male therapist that she had a sexual dream about him. But, she says, it is very difficult to relate this dream because "telling it to you would amplify it."

The fact is that, on the whole, patients in psychotherapy talk very little, spontaneously, to their therapists about them. It is extremely likely that the transformation of narrative content in this situation into an additional form of personal address contributes to the paucity of such content.[6] To some extent it surely is an effect of any face-to-face situation. In any event, that paucity is a fact.[7] Feelings and attitudes about other figures that might be expressed to the therapist in statements about them are more likely, when they involve the therapist, to be expressed in the quality of communication and interaction with him.

This thesis seems to me self-evident; however, it does not seem to be sufficiently appreciated. It is clear from psychoanalytic literature that the interpretation of transference reactions and attitudes, as it is practiced, relies primarily on the patient's allusions in the narrative or associative content to figures or relationships thought to stand for the therapist or for the relationship with him. The significance of the patient's actual behavior in his relations with the analyst is often noted in connection with the few moments during which the patient enters the office or departs; but once he begins to produce "material," in the traditional sense, it is the content of that production that seems almost exclusively to provide the basis for transference interpretation. The interpretive reliance on

---

[6]Gill also notes this fact. He points out, as a factor in the resistance to awareness of transference, "the difficulty in recognizing erotic and hostile impulses toward the very person to whom they have to be disclosed" (*Analysis of Transference* [1], vol. I, p. 59).

[7]Jean G. Schimek has suggested to me another possible factor in the patient's reluctance to talk about his reactions to the therapist, the expectable absence of reciprocity.

such content is another expression of the traditional preoccupation with text analysis, and it suffers from the usual deficiencies of that kind of analysis, as well as from some special ones.

Transference interpretations based solely on the patient's allusions to other figures (who might stand in a comparable relation to the patient) cannot be reliable. Even the possibility that a patient's unrecognized reaction to the therapist may be identical to the reaction he expresses at a particular time toward another figure—say, his boss—does not constitute unequivocal evidence that the one is a displacement of the other. On the contrary, if such reactions are derivatives or expressions of more general attitudes of the personality, their similarity in comparable circumstances is to be expected. The reactions to the boss and to the therapist may well be similar not because one is a displacement of the other but because both derive from the same general attitude toward figures who stand in a certain relation to the patient. (Essentially the same argument holds also for the interpretation of the attitude toward the therapist, as well as toward the boss, as standing for the attitude toward a childhood figure. In this case also a similarity of reaction may equally well be understood as deriving from a common attitude and evoked by subjectively comparable circumstances. This fact is no less true even if the earlier experience was important in the formation of that attitude.) A misinterpretation as a displacement of reaction of what is merely a similarity of reaction may retain a degree of plausibility, but it misidentifies the object of the patient's present interest or concern. Such an interpretation may gain a patient's "acceptance," but it will not enlarge his self-awareness.

The fact is that a displacement of reaction cannot be distinguished from a mere similarity on the basis of the content of particular references. This point reflects a general problem of interpretations based on particular textual contents alone. It is often not possible, on the basis of a particular textual reference (or, for that matter, the nature of a particular action) to determine its subjective significance. On that basis alone, it is often not possible to distinguish even between the subjectively important reference and the momentarily unimportant one or to determine whether or not the reference is made with particular interest in the person to whom it is made. It is not possible to determine, from a patient's consistent lateness in paying his bill, whether that act reflects primarily his attitude toward the therapist or toward money. And it is not possible to determine, from the fact that the patient's expressed attitude toward his boss may plausibly suit his relation with the therapist, which figure is at the moment on the patient's mind. Once again, the only way to make such determinations is to pay attention to the patient, not merely to his productions; in this case, to pay attention to how he talks to and how he behaves with the therapist.

There is, after all, a continuing interaction between patient and therapist from the time the patient enters the room. Some patients are acutely conscious of the presence of the therapist, although they may not realize it; others are much less so and are preoccupied with themselves or other concerns. Indeed, sometimes patients feel they should be more interested in the therapist than they are. For example, one twenty-two-year-old woman comes into the office with a greeting of particular deliberateness. She enters, turns slightly toward the therapist, and says, "How *are* you?" It turns out that she has felt "so self-indulgent" and has been concerned that she is insufficiently appreciative of the therapist.

Patient and therapist communicate constantly about a variety of arrangements. One patient, often sensitive about what she considers her low status, and pridefully determined to resist being "pushed around," seats herself, squints ostentatiously, and says, as if expecting an argument, "Would you *mind* adjusting that blind!"

Above all, it is simply in the course of talking, either about particular matters or in general, that various unrecognized attitudes and reactions to the therapist appear. Thus, a young man says, not just in a gloomy way, but with an embarrassed glance at the therapist, "It hasn't been such a good week." The therapist remarks that he seems sheepish about saying so. The patient replies, "You must be tired of hearing it." He feels that it is his responsibility to provide the therapist with a success.

The therapist talks in the therapy as well as the patient, and it should not be forgotten that his statements are also speech acts. The patient often responds to them as such, not only to their content. For some patients, to whom being a patient is already an indignity, each remark made about them by the therapist, not least if it is accurate, revives that indignity. For them it sometimes counts as the scoring of another point for the therapist.

One patient responds to an interpretation by the therapist with an ironic "Touché!" Another, somewhat similar person says, "Good work! You must have done your homework!" Yet another patient, not defensive but determined to understand and get the better of himself by himself, exclaims, "Why couldn't *I* have thought of that?" By contrast, it is well known that some patients understand each remark of the therapist to imply a prescription or accept every idea of his as a lesson to be learned.

At bottom, the reason that the therapist must pay attention not merely to what the patient says that may allude to the therapist, but to how the patient lives that relationship, is the general one about which I have said so much. In this case, too, the therapeutic material is the patient, not only what the patient provides. It is in how the patient lives that relationship with the therapist or, if he alludes to the therapist, in how he does so that we can see the dynamics of his subjective world expressed in action—if indeed that relationship is at the moment a focus of that dynamics, among all the matters that might be.

PART THREE

The Therapeutic Process

Chapter 6

The Psychology of Therapeutic Change

What constitutes therapeutic change? How does it occur? The aims of psychotherapy have been described in various ways: as growth; as self-actualization or the fulfillment of potentialities; as the achievement of maturity, productiveness, or genitality; not to mention, simply, as the relief or cure of symptoms. Some of these aims project a model, an image of ideal mental health. Perhaps such ideals are unavoidable, but they cannot be taken too seriously. They tend to be inspirational rather than descriptive, and they probably reflect the values of their times. Besides, they cannot be of any real help to the therapist. The work of therapy proceeds on a small scale and cannot be steered by such distant points of reference.

Therapeutic goals must be of a different, simpler kind. Psychotherapy is essentially a subtractive process, not an additive one; it aims to remove, not to augment.[1] It does not aim directly to increase self-esteem, but to diminish shame. It aims to increase interest in life, but in the indirect way of diminishing the subjective distress and preoccupation with self that interfere with interest in life. Psychotherapy aims, in general, to reduce or eliminate the distress and disability that are a consequence of the neurotic person's reaction against himself. It aims, therefore, to diminish or eliminate the self-estrangement that is a consequence of that reaction, to bring the person into contact with himself. In short, it aims simply to repair.

To achieve any such change in a lasting way is no small accomplishment, for it involves a change—if only a comparatively small adjustment—of personality, of attitude. In this respect early psychoanalysis was more optimistic in its expectations of success than therapists can be today. It is not only that we have been taught by experience that change comes slowly. There is also a theoretical recognition involved. The more particular and isolated the neurotic problem is believed to be, the faster and the more complete one can expect the cure to be. We know now that the neurotic problem is not a matter of a specific repressed conflict or memory but a distortion of the personality. This fact alone is sufficient to tell us that substantial change can be achieved only slowly and probably incompletely. The inherent stability of personality guarantees that. Only the workings of an essentially unstable or fluid organization could be significantly altered easily. If such a change is more difficult to achieve than its earlier conception

---

[1]Freud distinguished psychotherapy from hypnotic suggestion by noting Leonardo's comparison between the sculptor, who reveals a form by removing material, and the painter, whose work consists of applying material. Sigmund Freud, "On Psychotherapy" (1904), *Standard Edition*, 7:260 (London: Hogarth Press, 1953).

was thought to be, it is also more difficult to explain. After all, it must be not merely of a sort that relieves the effects of a specific noxious conflict but one that relieves the internal conflict-producing stresses of a personality organization. If any claim is made that this can be accomplished by introducing the patient to himself, that claim must surely be justified.

Self-Understanding

The idea that self-understanding is in some way liberating is a very old idea. Isaiah Berlin traces it back at least as far as Aristotle.[2] It is certainly one of the fundamental points on which therapists of many different views agree, for therapists have found (or think they have found) that this old idea applies to the cure of neurosis. But why should it? And if it does, how does it? Precisely what kind of self-understanding, if any, is effective in producing such change? For there is apparently more than one kind. What is meant, for example, by "intellectual" insight, a type of self-understanding that supposedly is not effective in producing such change, and "emotional" insight, which supposedly is?

Whatever the processes involved in the therapeutic kind of self-understanding may be, they do not seem to be educational processes in the ordinary sense. The kind of change that psychologists call therapeutic and philosophers have considered liberating is not the kind that comes merely with new information or additional facts. Mere information or facts, it seems, can produce only that kind of understanding that is called,

[2] Isaiah Berlin, "From Hope and Fear Set Free," in his *Concepts and Categories: Philosophical Essays* (Harmondsworth, Eng.: Penguin, 1981), pp. 173–98.

117

although quite vaguely, "intellectual" understanding, and results, at most, in some superficial change of *behavior;* whereas the sort of change we call therapeutic is supposed to involve changes of feeling and attitude. The sort of self-understanding that is thought to be liberating or therapeutic, in fact, is generally understood to involve not new information so much as a rediscovery of what was in some sense already known, an unearthing or reordering of what was already there. It is thought to involve a clarification of some aspect of mental or emotional life that had been unclear, unrecognized, or unconscious, yet had its effects. The notion is actually quite close to what is nowadays referred to in a political context as "raising consciousness."

It was Freud, of course, who gave the idea of mutative self-understanding a scientific content and therapeutic significance. He did so in his program of making conscious what had been repressed, thus depriving unconscious aims and fantasies of their unruly independence and bringing them under the civilizing influence and control of conscious judgment and attitude. In its classic form, this program referred simply to the cure of the estranged neurotic symptom through the recovery of its repressed childhood sources. But it is also a striking and clarifying idea in a more general sense, and it was made more general in the conception of enlarging the domain of the ego.[3] It offers a picture of restoring the integration of the individual and, in fact, of enlarging, through some kind of self-knowledge, the realm of self-direction or personal autonomy.[4]

[3]In Freud's well-known words, "Where id was, there ego shall be." Sigmund Freud, *New Introductory Lectures on Psychoanalysis* (1933) *Standard Edition,* 22:80 (London: Hogarth Press, 1964).

[4]See Sigmund Freud, *The Ego and the Id* (1927) *Standard Edition,* 22:80 (London: Hogarth Press, 1964): "Analysis does not set out to make pathological reactions impossible but to give the patient's ego *freedom* to choose" (italics in original).

The psychoanalytic idea was that the highly charged childhood wish or fantasy was preserved in its original form on account of its repressed and dissociated status. Once remembered and exposed to the atmosphere of adult consciousness, it would seem mere anachronism and its force would be dissipated. Thus, what makes this kind of self-knowledge liberating, and what distinguishes it from education, is exactly its negative nature. In contrast to educative knowledge, it does not add; it subtracts. It removes something: the power of previously repressed wishes and the necessity for their repression. It frees the individual from the tyranny of unknown wishes and anxieties that require costly defenses and drive him to behavior or reactions that are strange to him and even antagonistic to his conscious interests.

In one way or another, this concept of an infringement on the individual's autonomy by his own unconscious wishes—or at least by that which is dissociated from his sense of what he is and what he wants—has remained fundamental to all psychotherapy which relies on self-understanding or "insight" to achieve its results. This central idea of the transforming effect of a very specific kind of self-understanding will be developed in what follows.

Articulation of Subjective Experience

As I have said, it is the articulation—necessarily initiated by the therapist—of what is already subjectively experienced by the patient, though not recognized by him, that is therapeutically effective. The patient experiences a tension whose dim sensation threatens him. He reacts not with an effort to articulate that tension, but with an effort to dispel it. In fact, he can neither articulate it nor dispel it. This is the situation, a product of the restrictive dynamics of the neurotic personality, that the therapist confronts when he introduces the patient to himself.

The articulation of that tension, or of the patient's effort to dispel it, through the initiative of the therapist, has an effect that is not adequately described merely as "insight." Such an articulation, or "raising of consciousness," of a previously unarticulated feeling or aim *changes the person who experiences it*. It changes the person's experience of himself. Indeed, it changes his relation to himself in a specific way: symptomatic behavior that had been experienced passively comes to be experienced, when its aims or the subjective necessities that prompt it are articulated, as one's own, as purposeful and active. What was experienced as pressure is now experienced as purpose. With the transformation of unarticulated tension into consciously recognized feeling or aim, the person becomes, at least momentarily, more purposeful. That is to say, he becomes more completely integrated.

For example, a divorced woman in her twenties is often preoccupied with the rejection she suffered when her husband left her a year before for another woman. She describes, in her therapy hour, how she "can't get it out of my mind." On this occasion, she remembers the anniversary of a trip they took together. She cries as she speaks of it. Her tears are real; yet the way she revives the events in unhappy detail seems somewhat forced.

THERAPIST: You seem to rub it in.
PATIENT *(silent, then thoughtfully):* I'm facing facts.

The Psychology of Therapeutic Change

The transformation of passively experienced distress into an experience of active purpose, initiated in this case by the therapist and continued by the patient, is likely to come about in increments. The change illustrated is an initial step that raises, in turn, the possibility of further articulation of the nature and the objectives of such "facing facts." But each increment of the sense of purpose, however incomplete, will diminish the experience of pressure or passive distress. Even when the patient realizes no more than that she is doing something that she describes as "facing facts," her obsession no longer operates as reflexively as before. The transformation or "raising of consciousness" I am describing, it should be noted, has both a subjective and an objective aspect. It not only increases the sense of purposiveness but also increases the actuality of purposiveness. In other words, it raises the level of intentionality of symptomatic behavior. To the extent that aims become consciously articulated, action becomes—and feels—more intentional, and the individual may be described as more self-directing.[5]

Such advances in intentionality and awareness of purpose have two general effects that might seem paradoxical. On the one hand, past symptomatic behavior (which had been experienced as mysterious, accidental, failure of will, etc.) now seems to the patient to have been psychologically inevitable given his point of view and the existing circumstances. On the other hand, present and future behavior (which had seemed unpredictable and uncontrollable) now seem more volitional. These two effects have a common cause. Where before the individual was cut off from a sense of his own behavior's subjective necessity—hence also cut off from a sense of its author-

[5]See the discussion of the development of self-direction in chapter 2 of my *Autonomy and Rigid Character* (New York: Basic Books, 1981).

ship—now he is not. With an enlarged sense of authorship, past reactions seem understandable in light of his point of view at the time, while the present and future are seen to rest with his present and future aims. A gap in the chain of causality, as far as symptomatic behavior is concerned, is filled for both past and future by the individual's enlarged awareness of himself.

This advance in intentionality and restoration of the sense of authorship of one's own behavior clarifies the meaning of the frequently expressed idea that psychotherapy enlarges or restores choice. That idea cannot mean that psychotherapy makes it possible to choose what to want or not to want. No one can choose that. It can only mean that *knowing what one wants*, or what one wants to do, increases the deliberateness of action. It allows to a greater extent the contemplation of an action, or its objective, as against other possibilities. For this reason, as the sense of authorship of symptomatic action is enlarged, interest in that action may diminish.

The idea of the enlargement of intentionality, of the sense of authorship, and of choice in psychotherapy is, as I said, consistent with Freud's general conception of the enlargement, in analysis, of the domain of the ego. The enlargement specifically of the sense of authorship has been described in various ways. Kaiser, who emphasized its central place in the therapeutic process and in restoring the integrity of the personality, spoke of it as an enlargement of the patient's experience of "responsibility" for his actions.[6] Roy Schafer has spoken of the sense of being the "agent" of one's action with the same meaning.[7] I have described the experience in similar terms, but

---

[6] Hellmuth Kaiser, "The Problem of Responsibility in Psychotherapy," in *Effective Psychotherapy: The Contribution of Hellmuth Kaiser,* ed. L. B. Fierman (New York: Free Press, 1965), pp. 1–13.
[7] Roy Schafer, *The Analytic Attitude* (New York: Basic Books, 1983).

I consider it important also to emphasize that the subjective experience of authorship is an aspect of an actual advance in personal autonomy or self-direction.[8]

Polarization

The conscious articulation of previously estranged and unarticulated aims not only alters the individual's sense of himself and relation to himself. At the same time that his sense of himself is clarified, his experience of his world is also sharpened; specifically, the objectives of those aims and the situation to which they are responsive are brought into focus. In other words, an increased differentiation or, in Heinz Werner's term, polarity[9] between the self and the external situation is achieved by the articulation of subjective experience.

Consider this example: A highly educated and dignified elderly woman has been isolated and obviously lonely, despite a large circle of friends, since the death of her husband several years before. She is very prideful, however, and does not like to admit her loneliness. She has become a very heavy, though sporadic, drinker. In her first therapy hours, she makes no reference to any drinking problem. Now, she acknowledges such a problem but, like many heavy drinkers and drug users, she regards her bouts of drinking in a special way. She considers them to be impulsive, almost accidental acts, not really intentional despite their regularity. She says that she intends to have only a glass or two of sherry. But then she sometimes drinks

[8]See Shapiro, *Autonomy and Rigid Character* [5].

[9]Heinz Werner, *Comparative Psychology of Mental Development* (Chicago: Follett, 1948).

"more than I wanted to." At various times, she speaks of her drinking as a reflection of a moral weakness, a lack of will power, or even a lack of "common sense." She thinks of it as a failing, in other words, and she is repentant and disgusted with herself for this failing. But she never thinks of it as a wish or an intention to get drunk. In the following episode, however, after a drinking bout, she comes to a different realization.

PATIENT: All right, I suppose something *in* me, something *infantile*, wants to [drink], but *I* don't want to!

THERAPIST: You say "something infantile" quite contemptuously.

PATIENT: It *is* infantile! It's against my responsibility to my friends! It's an escape, it throws everything onto them.

THERAPIST: Perhaps there are times when escape seems necessary.

PATIENT *(angrily):* Are you saying I don't believe in my responsibilities to my friends?

THERAPIST: I am saying that sometimes one may not feel up to such responsibilities.

PATIENT *(becomes quiet, cries):* Oh, they're not really my friends. They were his friends, they see me out of duty. They don't give a damn about me . . . nor I, sometimes, about them.

The patient then goes on to speak of her isolation and loneliness since her husband's death and of her actual wish to drink and to "escape." She also talks more specifically about her relations with various of the friends in her old circle. The truth seems to be neither the complete mutual devotion she had always maintained nor the complete indifference she had just asserted. It is more complicated than either.

The Psychology of Therapeutic Change

What has happened to the patient in this episode? Her contact with herself—her awareness of the way she feels and what she wants to do—has been enlarged, and *she has been changed by this awareness*. At least for the time being, she has been changed from a person who feels driven to drink (either by accident or by "something infantile" in her) to a person with the conscious wish to drink; from someone who drinks without recognizing her own intention to someone who knows she wants to drink. An action that was experienced as accidental[10] is now experienced as intentional.

But there is a further element to the change. At the same time that her sense of her own action and of herself has been sharpened, the whole external situation to which that action was responsive has come into focus. The articulation of unrecognized purpose and the bringing into focus of the external situation to which that purpose is responsive cannot be separated. Together they constitute an advance in the polarization of the self and the external world.

The following is a simpler example. A young divorced woman is much concerned about getting married again and having children soon. She cannot comfortably allow herself to spend ("waste") her time alone, even if she enjoys it, or with a friend who is ineligible as a husband. She thinks she should, instead, be going to a bar where single people go to meet each other, but which she dislikes.

PATIENT *(somewhat agitated):* It's just that I keep thinking I'm wasting time! I could be going to [the singles bar] ... maybe I'd meet somebody! I'm thirty-two! I just read the statistics!

---

[10]For Schafer, "disclaimed action"; for Kaiser, an impaired sense of "responsibility" for action.

125

THERAPIST: You call what you do "thinking," but actually you nag yourself.

PATIENT *(quieter):* I hate that place. . . . Oh, I never meet anybody at these things anyway.

The process is the same, but in one respect it is even clearer in this example. Her original reference to the bar as a place where she might "meet somebody" is clearly less a representation of the bar than an expression of her reproachful nagging. Her attitude toward her own "wasting" of time and the vague idea of the singles bar are fused. The sharpened sense of herself achieved by the articulation of her nagging harassment simultaneously brings into more realistic focus the situation that is the objective of that nagging.

Once again, the therapeutic articulation of the unrecognized aims and feelings that prompt action or symptomatic behavior has the effect of restoring the sense of authorship of that behavior and raising its level of intentionality. But the patient in psychotherapy is also introduced to many kinds of estranged and unrecognized subjective experience—feelings, attitudes, ideas, interests, and concerns—which do not directly involve action or intentions. Such feelings, of course, have objects—they are about something—but they do not necessarily directly involve doing something. The effects of articulating such kinds of subjective experience are much the same. The sense of the self is sharpened and, at the same time, the polarity between the self and the external object or situation of interest is increased. For instance, the therapeutic recognition of an emotional reaction that has been denied—"hurt" feelings in the following example—simultaneously brings into more realistic focus the object of those feelings. In that sense the emotional relationship between the individual and the object of his feeling is changed by the conscious articulation of that emotional reaction. One might almost say that a relationship is created, where before there was only the reaction of an egocentric sensitivity to an event.

The process is apparent in the following case. A thirty-five-year-old chemist, a rather paranoid man of exceedingly sensitive pride, is frequently, loudly, angry. He often rails at his superiors, as he does on this day. His anger, however, is usually defensive. His railing, though he does not realize it, is very much a roar of wounded pride.

PATIENT *(referring to his superiors):* The dunces! . . . Stuffy hidebound bastards! They're afraid to recognize me! . . . I'm a threat to them! I'm too smart for them. They're way behind me. . . . I'll quit, that's all! . . .

THERAPIST *(after a time interrupts):* You haven't said what happened.

PATIENT: Oh, just these old fools . . . got ahead by seniority and don't want to let any new blood in, any young ideas. They can't stand it because I'm vigorous and they're half dead. . . . *(The picture gradually emerges that the patient has approached his boss with a suggestion and has been politely sent back to his immediate superior. He continues):* They can't stand a creative young guy! Bureaucrats! . . . *(He contemptuously describes various of his superiors' foolish habits.)* . . . they're senile. . . . Believe me, they're fools! . . .

THERAPIST *(interrupts):* Perhaps they are fools, as you say, but for fools, you certainly don't take them lightly.

PATIENT: What do you mean?

THERAPIST: I mean that it seems to be very important to you whether they appreciate you or not.

PATIENT *(much quieter):* Well . . . J. [his immediate superior] *is* a fool. . . . L. [the boss] is pretty smart.

THERAPIST: Maybe he's the one who upset you.

PATIENT: Wouldn't *you* be?

THERAPIST: Perhaps I would. Then we would both be very sensitive to such things.

PATIENT: Everybody needs recognition.

THERAPIST: That's true, but to some it's a much more serious matter than to others.

PATIENT: It's my boss! I want a raise, it's important what he thinks of me!

THERAPIST: You're saying that it's just a practical matter?

PATIENT *(silent; looks softer, even wistful):* Well, I admit my feelings were probably hurt.

THERAPIST: Do you mean "were" or "are"?

PATIENT: All right, I admit it, *are.*

THERAPIST: What's there to "admit" about hurt feelings?

PATIENT *(briefly angry again):* It kills me that these nothings can hurt my feelings!

The patient then further "admits," quietly, though still grudgingly, that several days ago, though he "forgot" to mention it, he had asked the boss to join him at a coffee break but had been, again apparently politely, refused.

This episode contains a striking change in the patient. Initially, he was defensively angry, railing against his bosses, discrediting them, and proclaiming his own superiority. By the end of the hour, he says almost the reverse. Where he was loud and angry before, he is now quiet and wistful. Where he insisted on his own superiority and their insignificance, now he "admits" his respect for at least one of them, his wish to win their acceptance, and his "hurt" feelings, probably humiliation, on being rebuffed. It is true, of course, that his inflated and essentially artificial dignity still makes it a very hard pill to swallow; the fact of hurt feelings itself is humiliating for him to recognize ("admit"). It is true, in other words, that the change is far from complete and in fact, by the end of this episode, it is partially undone. Yet, as far as it goes, it is a real change and a dynamic one. A process of self-deception, a defense, has been relaxed, if only for the time being and with obvious ambivalence. In place of an artificial, strident, and defensive arrogance, there is a genuineness and awareness of his own feelings. The patient has been brought into greater contact with himself.

These changes need to be considered more closely. What is the difference between the man who does not know his feelings are hurt and the man who does? What, indeed, do we mean by feeling hurt and not knowing it? Is the difference between the two conditions one that can account for this dynamic change?

We are always somewhat at a loss to describe the quality of a subjective experience that is unarticulated. It is comparable in some ways to the difficulty of imagining the subjective experience of infants, though compared to that problem our case offers some firmer ground. We have assumed that even as this patient is railing at his superiors and contemptuously discrediting them, some form of experience of "hurt" and humiliation, some sort of ashamed self-conscious awareness of their rebuff, continues to smart. This much is something more than mere conjecture. We hear the distress in his voice even when his words are dismissive. We know from what he tells us that self-conscious thoughts about his bosses' image of him are very much on his mind ("They're afraid to recognize me," etc.). And we can see no other reasonable explanation for his repeated declarations of his own superiority than the effort to dispel a sensation of humiliation and inferiority, which has been aroused by his subordinate status and intensified by their rebuff. He tells us later that such feelings "kill" him. One can only imagine such feelings, before they are articulated, to consist of fragmentary idea-sensations, perhaps not unlike those in dreams. They may be idea-sensations, for example, in which the feeling of humiliation or of one's own inferiority is embedded in the image of the other's smugness; or in which contempt for oneself is contained in fragmentary recollections—or revivals of the sensation—of a rebuff, of what the other one said, or of how the other one looked. We imagine, in other words, a fusion of the "hurt" and humiliated feelings on the one hand, with the figure who triggered those feelings on the other. It is ultimately only such a fusion that can account for the intensity of the patient's reaction to that figure.

The effect of articulating such feelings is, once again, the dual effect of an increased polarity between self and object. The sense of the self is clarified, and feelings take more definite form and direction; at the same time, the object of those feelings comes into focus. For what may have seemed a sharply focused object of the original reaction, in this case the patient's superiors, was in reality not so. The patient's superiors, or more precisely the rebuff at their hands, was merely the trigger, a signal of bossness, a sharp and humiliating reminder of others' superiority, or (its subjective equivalent) of one's own inferiority. The figure of the boss was no more a true focus or object of the patient's reaction than a hot dish from which one has just flinched in pain can be said to be the focus of that pain. One may curse the dish, but the pain is its own focus. The patient's immediate reaction is of that sort: an essentially egocentric reaction, a painful sensitivity aggravated by a sharp abrasion. What he says about his superiors is not so much an expression of his perceptions of them as it is an expression of how they make him feel. Only when that undifferentiated idea-sensation of humiliating smallness-before-their-bigness is articulated and thereby transformed into *a feeling of his* does the trigger of that feeling—the boss—emerge as an objective figure. It is at that point that the patient can be said to have an attitude toward him and a relationship with such a figure ("Well, L. is pretty smart . . . J. is a fool"). Self and object differentiate out of an egocentric merging of the two.

How does the emergence of this new experience, this sharpened polarity, change the dynamic situation? In other words, how does that increased polarity affect the workings of the consciousness-distorting attitudes of the neurosis? It seems evident that it does. But why should it?

To understand the effects of articulating the dynamics of subjective experience one need only remember the nature of those dynamics. Specifically, one need only remember that it is precisely its estranged, unarticulated, and therefore comparatively undifferentiated, nature that accounts for the neurotic dynamics of subjective experience. This is what accounts for its largely reflexive operation. It is the essentially unarticulated and undifferentiated nature of certain feelings and aims—the fact that awareness of them is only vague and incipient, global and without proportion—that makes their sensation as threatening as it is. Thus a circularity is established in the workings of neurotic personality: the restrictive dynamics of the personality prevents the articulation of certain aspects of subjective experience; the unarticulated discomfort or threat of that subjective sensation, in turn, propels this dynamics. It is this circularity that is responsible for the irreversibility of the neurotic process without external intervention.

But now an external agency in the person of the therapist intervenes and initiates what cannot be initiated spontaneously. The therapist initiates the articulation that would otherwise be reflexively avoided. Why, then, does the patient not immediately shrink from this action by the therapist? In fact, we know that to a certain extent he does. We know that the therapist's action typically meets with discomfort, confusion, objection, or temporizing on the patient's part ("What do you mean?"; "Are you saying . . . ?"; "That's impossible!"). The newly articulated aim or feeling meets with an immediate reaction that resembles the reaction to the unarticulated sensation of it. But following that initial discomfort—once over the hump, so to speak—there is a change. For what had been unassimilable as a vague, unarticulated sensation becomes at least partially assimilable as an articulated feeling, aim, or idea. As soon as the chemist in the example just cited says, or thinks in an articulated way, "My feelings were hurt [by him]," his experience has taken a different and more assimilable form. In its previous form of global, diffuse idea-sensation of no definite size or proportion, the humiliation had reflexively triggered a defensive and arrogant roar. Now, the experience of the articulated feeling and the real figures no longer prompts such a reaction; that reaction becomes exorbitant, disproportionate, unnecessary. This change does not mean, of course, that the neurotic conflict is thereby resolved and the personality permanently changed. It cannot be resolved so easily because far more is contained in that conflict and in the attitudes involved in it than what has been articulated in the single instance. But it does constitute an effect on that personality and its consciousness-distorting attitudes that may not be entirely lost.

Reaction to the Self

There is one category of the neurotic person's feelings and reactions whose articulation warrants some further and specific consideration here: his unrecognized feelings and attitudes toward himself. Everything that has been said in general concerning the articulation of feelings, motivations, and attitudes in general holds also when their object is the patient himself. The effects of the articulation of his reactions to himself are just the same: he feels a clearer sense of his own feelings, while at the same time the object of those feelings—himself—comes into more objective focus.

Thus the patient becomes aware in a particular connection, as he was not before, that he *has* an attitude, or attitudes, about himself. He may even realize that he is preoccupied with himself. He may become aware that he disapproves of himself, is ashamed of himself; that he thinks he is selfish or dishonest, or weak and unmanly; or, more likely, that he thinks he might be or might appear to be, and must watch himself carefully in order to avoid it. To the extent that such feelings and attitudes are unarticulated, they will be fused with their object or the events that trigger them. Thus, the effects of such unarticulated attitudes about the self will be experienced in the impact of a personal event—perhaps some success or failure—in a concern about some feature of personal image, or in the quality of concern about a particular person's reaction to oneself. In other words, the *effects* of such feelings and attitudes toward the self will be experienced in the personal circumstances of life and will be a determinant of behavior, but without the patient's awareness of the source of these effects.

For example, a thirty-seven-year-old divorced man, who has

been depressed, is nervous about asking a certain young woman for a date and has avoided doing so. He recognizes that she has behaved in a such way as to make it clear that she would welcome an invitation. He is quite presentable, though he may look a few years older than his age. But he is very conscious of looking older and of some old acne scars. An attitude toward himself is, at the moment, to some extent expressed in this self-consciousness, but most acutely in his concern with the possibility of "rejection."

> PATIENT: I don't know, I guess I'm afraid of rejection. She's quite good-looking. She must get plenty of offers.
> THERAPIST: You mean, maybe, *you're* not in her class.
> PATIENT *(with slight irony):* She might think, "Where does this ugly old creep come off asking me out?"
> THERAPIST: *She* might think?
> PATIENT *(laughs)*

Thus, the therapist begins to articulate the patient's attitude toward himself (*"you're* not in her class"). One effect of this articulation is that the vague but inhibiting "fear of rejection" that had been experienced as emanating from *her* is transformed into an awareness of *his* feeling that the invitation would be an act of presumption. At the same time, his image of himself ("this ugly, old creep") starts to come into focus, though still diminished in clarity by its ironic exaggeration. In other words, a polarity begins to emerge: the patient acquires some awareness of his attitude to himself; and this sense of his attitude begins to bring into focus, however disproportionately, the object of that attitude, himself. Initial objectifications of the self are often disproportionate because the previous fragmentary images and sensations of the self, in consequence of being unarticulated and reactive to passing circumstances, are typically extreme and unstable. The moment that this patient's attitude to himself and idea of himself begin to materialize out of the vague, relatively undifferentiated matrix of "fear of rejection," therefore, is not a happy one. Even so, it is an advance over the previous status of these feelings. For, once his attitude to himself is articulated to any degree and a picture of himself begins to come into focus, the possibility for further, more proportioned consideration of it exists.

A patient may be introduced not only to such feelings and attitudes about himself but also to various more complicated reactions prompted by those feelings, particularly his reactive efforts to dispel them. For example, he may be introduced to the fact that he measures himself constantly; that his estimation of himself rises and falls radically with his latest success or failure or the most recent smile or frown from his audience; or that he monitors, nags, or harasses himself. He will have experienced the effects of that harassment, the fluctuating *results* of those measurements, but without awareness that it is his own reactions to himself, prompted by his own attitudes, that produce those effects. In short, he may be introduced to various aspects of the dynamics of his subjective reaction to himself. The articulation of those reactions will have, again, the additional result of a more objective and more stable image of himself.

For example: A dignified, soft-spoken businessman in his fifties originally sought therapy because of a severe depression triggered by circumstances unrelated to the matter now at hand. After some months, he feels generally somewhat better, but on this occasion he arrives for his hour with a severe, determined expression. The time has come, he says, that he wishes to talk about certain things that he has not disclosed to anyone for many years, not even to members of his own family. He then quietly describes—admits—certain business and personal deceptions and, in his view, acts beneath his professed standards of behavior, which he committed many years ago during a serious crisis in the family business. Ashamed, he has never disclosed these things in the intervening years, and hiding them has sometimes required further deceptions, even in his relations with those close to him.

He concludes his story by saying softly that he has always wished to think of himself as an honorable man but clearly cannot do so, for he was certainly dishonorable in this matter and, by hiding it, has continued to be so to this day. He looks at the therapist, it seems, anxiously.

The therapist, in recognition of this glance, says that despite the patient's statement, his judgment seems to be in some doubt. The patient replies, "Not really," adding that he sees "no other conclusion." The therapist suggests that even this remark is not made quite conclusively, but rather as if the patient thinks it to be the judgment he *should* accept.

The discussion continues. It is apparent—and in the course of the exchange the therapist says as much—that the patient has wrestled for years with the charges he brings against himself, continually reviewing the evidence. For years, he has held hearings, as it were, without being aware that he was doing so. On the evidence of these events, he has not been able to acquit himself with the verdict "Honorable." But he obviously has not been willing either to accept the equally absolute verdict "Dishonorable." So, this internal court always recesses inconclusively, to be resumed shortly.

After a moment, he proceeds to tell, in more simple language, of the actual circumstances of the business crisis, his extreme fears at the time for his own and his family's future, and the actions he was prompted to take by these circumstances and fears. A more realistic picture of himself emerges, one that is neither totally honorable nor totally dishonorable but is, in fact, less remarkable than either. His previous idea of himself probably fluctuated between the two extremes, but remained essentially vague and uneasy as he tried to sustain one image and dispel the other. The articulation of that continued effort permits its object, himself, to come into more realistic focus.

Development of Self-Awareness in Childhood

The polarizing effects of the therapeutic articulation of subjective experience are consistent with fundamental developmental processes, particularly with the child's development of conscious motives and the objectification of his world. I do not mean to suggest that therapeutic change in the adult is in some way modeled on the developmental prototype, but simply that the same basic psychological processes operate in both.

The subjective world of the infant is not, in the beginning, a world of conscious aims and purposes, or of objective figures and things about which he has attitudes and feelings.[11] Although it seems that some sort of infantile distinction between sensations of internal and external origin is present almost from the beginning,[12] essentially the new infant reacts to his own sensations. He reacts more or less reflexively to need-relevant or instinctive response-relevant cues; or a little later, to familiar

[11]Werner, *Comparative Psychology* [9], esp. pp. 191ff.
[12]See Daniel N. Stern, *The Interpersonal World of the Infant* (New York: Basic Books, 1985).

cues whose "feel" triggers various more differentiated, but still basically instinctive, reactions. For instance, the approach of the bottle triggers sucking and anticipation. But this reaction does not demonstrate an infantile concept of an independently existing bottle-thing. At this point, one cannot speak of feelings about or attitudes to things or people, or of fully reflectively conscious aims, or of genuinely intentional action. All of these presume a degree of differentiation or polarity between the self and the objective world that does not yet exist.

Only gradually, in the course of activity, experience, and development, including language development, does the world become objectified. Where there were only "things-of-action" there are now "objects of contemplation."[13] Durable and specific feelings and attitudes about the world develop and become articulated, as does the child's awareness of himself. He not only reacts but knows what he wants and what he wants to do. The child's relation to the world changes with this polarity, and so does his relation to himself. Passively triggered and immediate reaction is increasingly superseded by consciously purposeful and intentional, self-directed, action which grows out of the imagination of possibilities.[14] The conditions are established for a sense of authorship of action and a sense of choice.

In this development, as Heinz Werner and Bernard Kaplan put it, "with the attainment of higher levels, lower levels are not lost."[15] Passively experienced, unarticulated reactiveness is never completely displaced by clearly articulated feelings and aims even though, as far as significant action is concerned, such

13Heinz Werner and Bernard Kaplan, *Symbol Formation* (New York: Wiley, 1963), pp. 67ff.
14See Shapiro, *Autonomy and Rigid Character* [5], chap. 2.
15Werner and Kaplan, *Symbol Formation* [13], p. 8.

reactiveness becomes subordinate to conscious purposes. All sorts of fragmentary, egocentric and syncretic, unarticulated idea-sensations continue to surround articulated, fully conscious feelings, interests, and purposes. And in fact it is reasonable to assume that all consciously articulated feelings, ideas, and purposes continue to be formed out of a matrix of unarticulated subjective experience and that they undergo a "microgenesis,"[16] however rapidly, through stages of unarticulated and vaguely articulated sensation and reaction before achieving conscious articulation. In this sense, it can be said that the condition—even the discomforting condition—of not knowing what one feels or wants to do is a normal and inevitable condition of life, if it is more or less transient. That transient condition is normally relieved spontaneously; feelings are clarified, ideas and conscious purposes are formed, and objectives come into focus often with the help of language, sometimes by "talking it out." It is not catharsis, but the articulation of subjective experience, that is the normal "therapeutic" value of talking.

For example, a businessman describes, with some concern, a certain transaction of his partner's. Finally, reluctantly, he expresses some doubts about this man's honesty. Then he adds, "I always knew it. But you don't *really* know it until you say it publicly."

If it is so that feelings, ideas, and purposes are normally spontaneously formed and integrated with the personality in this way, then we can perhaps think of psychotherapy as a systematic procedure that restores the capacity for such articulation where the restrictive and self-estranging neurotic personality has consistently prevented it.

[16]Ibid., esp. p. 18.

Chapter 7

The Therapeutic
Relationship

It is sometimes said that what really matters in psychotherapy, what determines its success or failure, is not the theoretical orientation of the therapist, the method that he follows or thinks he follows, but the quality of the relationships he establishes with his patients. Thus, Kaiser concluded that the therapist's communicative attitude was the effective therapeutic agent.[1] That view goes too far. I have tried to show that, under certain conditions, the communication of certain sorts of ideas will have therapeutic effects, while others will not. There is good reason to believe in general that ideas can affect people. Yet, even if it is not true that the quality of the therapeutic relationship is the only thing that matters to the effectiveness

[1] Hellmuth Kaiser, "The Universal Symptom of the Psychoneuroses: A Search for the Conditions of Effective Psychotherapy," in *Effective Psychotherapy: The Contribution of Hellmuth Kaiser,* ed. L. B. Fierman (New York: Free Press, 1965), pp. 152ff.

of psychotherapy, there is no doubt that it does matter in some important way. Even apart from the quality of that continuing relationship, the very communication of the idea itself must be considered. Ideas are not transferred metaphysically. Every statement of an idea by the therapist, no less than by the patient, is at the same time an action and, insofar as it is a communication of some sort, a social action. That communication in itself expresses a purpose, an attitude, a relationship as well as an idea. I shall try to show that, in fact, those therapeutic communications which are effective do express not only an idea but also a certain sort of relationship and attitude toward the patient.

Contact with the Self and Contact with the Therapist

We have already encountered clinical observations and even a general principle that indicate a significant correspondence between the quality of the therapeutic relationship on the one hand and the patient's neurotic condition on the other. In chapter 5 I summarized these observations in the principle that the patient's neurotic self-estrangement and self-deception invariably distort his communication with the therapist. It is true that this correspondence does not seem at first to satisfy our interest; for it describes the effect of the patient's condition on the quality of the relations between patient and therapist, rather than the reverse. But it is a correspondence that is worth considering further and will yield a significant result.

The correspondence may in fact easily be extended. In every single case I have mentioned, when the patient is brought into greater contact with himself, with his actual feelings and thoughts, there is at the same time an increased contact with the therapist.

Consider again the case I have cited:

PATIENT *(with exaggerated confidence):* I'm sure it's the right thing to do! . . . I guess.

THERAPIST: You *guess.*

The patient is surprised, starts to object, then laughs. He proceeds to describe his doubts, talking now in a quieter way.

It is evident that the therapist experiences a greater contact, a more genuine communication with the patient when he talks about his doubts than when he is stridently denying them. It is easy to understand. When the neurotic person is cut off from his actual feelings and engaged in the very process of deceiving himself, he cannot at the same time communicate genuinely with the therapist. On the contrary, he must avoid contact with him, in one way or another, in order to avoid encountering himself. As the example makes plain, the patient's effort to deny his feelings transforms his talking into something other than genuine communication; it becomes a speech act of a different kind, an instrument of self-deception. But at the same time that this transformation has internal, consciousness-distorting effects, it is bound to affect the relationship with the other.

Perhaps the patient talks, as in this example, as if he were making a speech, trying to persuade or exhort, speaking more loudly, more forcefully than he would otherwise. Perhaps he looks not so much *at* the therapist as, in a special, urgent way, *for a sign from* him, for assurance or confirmation. Perhaps he plugs away dutifully, without interest in or conviction about what he is saying, avoiding meeting the therapist's glance altogether. The examples could be multiplied. What they have in common is what is absent in all of them. In all such instances, the patient is not talking to the therapist, but is doing something else. And the therapist, for his part, will experience that absence of communication, though he may not recognize it for what it is. In that case, the therapist, attempting to attend to what the patient is saying as if it were genuine communication, is likely to find himself bored and restless. By contrast, when the patient is able, in the example as a result of the therapist's intervention, to "be himself," he can also talk *to* the therapist genuinely and with conviction. And, as a rule, then, he wants to do so.

Now, these considerations raise an interesting question: if diminishing the patient's estrangement from himself also diminishes his estrangement from the therapist and permits a greater communicative contact with him, might the effect also be produced in the other direction? Might the achievement of a more genuinely communicative relationship with the therapist simultaneously diminish the patient's estrangement from himself? If it were so, might we not achieve our aim of bringing the patient into greater contact with himself by establishing a more genuine and communicative contact with him?

Logically, the inference is persuasive. As a guide to the therapist, however, it seems of doubtful value. In fact, it may merely be a question-begging restatement of the problem. For it is after all precisely the patient's existing condition of neurotic self-estrangement that interferes with and distorts the therapeutic relationship from his side and constitutes an obstacle to such communicative contact. The therapeutic situation may offer the patient the opportunity for a more communicative relationship, but the patient, precisely because of the nature of his problem, cannot be expected accept it. How can one establish such contact with a person whose own subjective dynamics makes it intolerable and requires that he avoid it? How can one establish such genuinely communicative relations with someone, say, who must convince himself—and therefore must convince you as well—that he feels more confident than he does, or more manly; or with someone whose subjective dynamics requires him to talk dutifully and monotonously about what he himself is not interested in, though he is trying to believe that he is? Are we not then back at the beginning?

Not entirely. Certainly these considerations discourage any hopes for a shortcut to the therapeutic goal. Still, if the idea— that communicative contact with the therapist will, at the same time, mean the patient's achievement of contact with himself—does not offer a shortcut to therapeutic change, it can still offer something more limited. At least, it will help us to recognize the presence and understand the significance of the therapeutic relationship in such change as does occur.

Besides, it is not as difficult as one might imagine to find instances in which the therapeutic relationship, by itself, has much the effect I suggested of bringing the patient into contact with himself, at least momentarily. In the instances I have in mind, there is no verbalization whatever—I do not say no communication—on the therapist's part.

For example, an ambitious and quite successful executive often measures and worries over the quality of his life. He is very conscious of his immigrant family's status, and he rails against the "old-boys network" that he feels excludes him from the highest executive levels and limits him to less than a "first-class" life. He is determined not to "settle" for that status, not to be "a happy idiot." He is therefore extremely reluctant to "admit" any satisfaction and often reminds himself of his frustrations, exaggerating them with a kind of worked-up outrage. He has changed, however, in the course of the therapy. At this point, when he exaggerates his problems and searches for new ways to express his moral outrage, he sometimes has to laugh at his own excesses. But he still does not like to laugh and does not want to.

> PATIENT *(enters, seats himself with an exaggerated sigh):* Well, another week in this rotten, second-class career. . . . Did I say career? Job! Day labor! . . . Luckily it probably won't go on long. . . . *(He continues, speaking of the supposed likelihood of his being fired.)*

The therapist says nothing but is aware, as the patient is not, at this point, that this scene is not authentic tragedy. Perhaps, without an intention to do so, the therapist has some look of skepticism or amusement.

> PATIENT *(glances at therapist, starts to laugh quite genuinely, and is obviously struggling against it):* You're making me laugh!
> THERAPIST: I?
> PATIENT: Yes, I can see the look on your face, I can see you're amused, that's why I'm laughing!
> THERAPIST: Do you really think that if you were in the midst of such unhappiness, a look on my face would be enough to make you laugh?
> PATIENT *(momentarily confused, flustered, relaxes):* Well, I guess I do get a little carried away.

He then "admits" that something quite satisfying has happened and, still nervous and grudging, talks about it.

This incident seems, at least in a limited way, to confirm the

145

hypothesis I suggested. The therapist recognized, when the patient did not, the patient's estrangement from his actual feelings. Although the therapist had not intended as yet to communicate this recognition and was not attempting to do so, he did not feel and was not attempting to assume an expression of sympathy. The patient may well have seen a look of doubt or amusement in the therapist's eyes. The patient's response, in turn, to what he saw in the therapist's face was involuntary and unwilling, a discomforting surprise to the patient himself. The response, in other words, met with the same initial resistance and confusion that any therapeutic articulation of an estranged feeling might. Nevertheless, the patient responded with a genuine feeling to the therapist's apparent recognition of the existence of such a feeling. This involuntary response led immediately to the patient's reluctant recognition of the nature of his actual feeling. There is no doubt that the patient's involuntary *social response* to the therapist, to the communicative contact between them, occurred momentarily before the patient's conscious recognition of the nature of his feeling.[2] Thus the therapeutic relationship may be said to have had the effect here of bringing the patient into contact with himself.

Comparable instances with similar results are not rare. They are not limited to situations that contain a potentially shared amusement. For example, a patient vigorously attempts to deny some distress or to give assurances, without conviction,

---

[2]It is entirely possible for such contact to occur before either patient or therapist consciously recognizes the nature of the patient's feelings. Veikko Tähkä's useful distinction between "complementary reactions" (immediate emotional reactions to another person's verbal and nonverbal messages) and empathic responses is relevant here. The patient's response to the therapist is certainly of the "complementary" sort while the therapist's unverbalized reaction to the patient is probably a mingling of the two. See Veikko Tähkä, "The Early Formation of the Mind," *International Journal of Psychoanalysis* 68 (1987): 229–50.

that some concern of his is groundless; as he tries in this way to persuade himself that all is well, he glances at the therapist. At the moment that he meets the therapist's eyes, he becomes flustered and cannot continue his speech. A moment later he becomes aware, at first reluctantly and uncomfortably, of the distress or concern that he had attempted to deny.

But, before one overestimates the power to defeat self-deception with such an involuntary communicative reaction, one must recognize that it can apparently occur only under very limited conditions. It appears that the effect can occur only if the patient's rejection of his estranged feeling is at that moment not intense. Otherwise the sensation of enlarged self-awareness will be discomforting enough to trigger a corrective reaction; the patient's avoidance of contact with the therapist will become more complete. For example, he will renew his speech with more determination than before or will avoid meeting the therapist's glance.

There is another element to the example of the patient who unwillingly laughs. Immediately afterward, he makes a complaint that, actually, is not at all rare in connection with such incidents: this never happens, he says, anywhere else. Never when he is alone, never with other people, not even with friends. Only here does he laugh about such things, he says. The implication is clear that his reaction here must therefore be considered an aberration and an event of doubtful validity, a laugh that is somehow not a laugh. Once again, then, he attempts to resume his sober expression. Once again, however, he looks at the therapist and starts, good-naturedly, to laugh.

The patient's complaint is based on valid observations, and it is instructive in two ways. The first is suggested by his remark that "this" never happens when he is alone. His remark reminds us that, however easily the neurotic self-deception may appear to have been abandoned in the therapeutic situation, it cannot as a rule be comparably abandoned spontaneously; the process of therapeutic change is an interpersonal process, a communicative process. The second point concerns the difference between what occurs when the patient is with his friends and what has occurred with the therapist. We can only conjecture, of course. Let us suppose that his friends feel obliged to take what he says and this picture that he sometimes presents of himself at face value. They may not recognize, or may only sense dimly and uncomfortably and perhaps try to overlook, the exaggerations and the forced, artificial quality of his gloom. Or—perhaps more likely—they recognize the exaggerations but feel obliged out of affection or politeness to treat them gingerly, perhaps with reassurances. But it is unlikely, however much affection they may feel for him in general, that they can actually share the concerns or actually feel sympathy for the picture of himself that he presents on such an occasion. He does not believe it himself, after all, and the instinctive sympathetic response to another person's emotional state is simply not likely to be aroused by that picture.

Therapists in comparable circumstances may react in a similar fashion. In their concern to feel—or to show—a sympathetic interest in the patient, therapists may fail to recognize that the picture the patient presents of himself is forced or exaggerated, in some way artificial, an act of self-deception. In this sense, the therapist's concern to feel a proper sympathy will work against the interests of the therapy. Such therapeutic situations achieve only a semblance of communication between the patient and the therapist: the patient does not actually believe in the picture of himself that he presents, while the therapist does not actually feel the sympathetic interest he expresses for it. By contrast, the recognition of the patient's exaggeration and the appreciation of its genuine subjective necessity make possible a true sympathetic response, even though in this case that response will initially consist of a shared laugh, to a degree, admittedly, at the patient's own expense.

I have attempted to isolate, through this example, a therapeutic effect of a certain kind of relationship in the absence of verbal communication. Obviously this is a special case, and it is not one that offers any special advantages; but the point I wish to make is general. In the example, the therapist's silent, but evidently communicative recognition of the patient's feeling—his "contact" with that feeling—which the patient himself did not recognize, evoked first a response and then conscious articulation of the feeling itself. As a general rule, however, this process is likely to be aborted in the absence of further verbal articulation by the therapist. The immediate response to the therapist is in itself insufficient to lead to a decisive enlargement of self-awareness in the face of the discomfort accompanying that self-awareness. Nevertheless, it seems that such a response to the therapist must be counted as a tendency that contributes to the raising and articulation of consciousness. Such a contact on the part of the therapist, and the patient's response to it, are fundamental to effective therapeutic communication, verbal or nonverbal. Such contact is the essential feature of the therapeutic relationship.

From this standpoint, the distinction between the nonverbal response of the therapist in my example and the more common verbal articulation by the therapist is not a sharp one. A verbal communication by the therapist, like the nonverbal one, may initiate contact with some feeling of the patient unrecognized by him.

Consider again, for example, a case cited in chapter 4 in

which the therapist said very little. The patient, trying conscientiously to respect the possibility that she may "really want" to continue her pregnancy and have another baby, describes her feeling when she sees a friend's baby:

> PATIENT *(emphatically, with a somewhat forced emotion):*
> . . . it looked wonderful. . . . It almost makes me feel like going ahead.
> THERAPIST: "Almost"?
> PATIENT *(momentarily flustered, then exclaiming):* Why don't I want another baby? Any normal woman would! It's not normal!

Here the therapist communicates his recognition of the patient's reservation, which the patient herself, in the process of self-deception, does not at the moment recognize. This communication evokes in turn a response—though probably a reluctant and discomforted one—of a previously unrecognized feeling from the patient. It is worth noting again that such a communication by the therapist evokes a response from the patient that initially is involuntary. The therapist's communication commands the patient's interest. It may not please her, indeed it may discomfort her; but it interests her. Furthermore, it does not result merely in a silent raising of consciousness, but prompts a communicative response consisting of a further articulation of the originally unrecognized thought or feeling. We are justified in saying, in other words, that the patient's articulation of her previously unrecognized thought or feeling develops in the course of her continued communicative response to the therapist. The communicative contact initiated by the therapist has been, in turn, enlarged by the patient, and this enlargement of communication between the two leads directly to an enlargement of the patient's self-awareness. The patient makes contact with the therapist and with herself at the same stroke.[3]

The Therapeutic Attitude

In a sense, the less said about a therapeutic attitude the better. To recommend to the therapist an attitude of a certain kind to his patients may only burden him with a self-conscious role. A therapeutic attitude must grow out of an understanding of both the work itself and the patient. Still, it may be useful to consider more explicitly the general attitude that is implied in the therapeutic view I am advocating, to examine its therapeutic significance and to distinguish it from other possibilities.

The therapist is not a mind reader. True, he may occasionally have a guess—quite likely a wrong one—about a specific thought or feeling that the patient does not himself recognize and cannot articulate. But on the whole he cannot see very far or very deep, and is more likely to be surprised at the newly articulated turn of the patient's thought or feeling than to have predicted it. The therapist encounters the patient's subjective world fully and clearly, as the patient himself does, only bit by bit, as it is articulated. Yet it is the therapist who initiates this process and sustains it. His observations and communications,

[3]Kaiser, who coined the phrase "communicative contact," came to the conclusion that such experience of communication was of therapeutic benefit and a therapeutic aim in itself (Kaiser, "Universal Symptom" [1], pp. 152ff.). My own conclusion is different. I easily see the satisfaction of the experience of communication with another person, but not in itself the therapeutic benefit. What is clear, however, is the enlargement of the patient's self-awareness in the course of communication with the therapist.

which recognize only a little more of the patient than the patient himself can see, are what interest the patient and make further articulation by the patient possible.

Consider in this light the example I cited a moment ago. The patient refers, with a rather forced enthusiasm, to a scene of mothering she had recently seen: "It almost made me want to go ahead!" The therapist repeats, "Almost?" The patient, after a few moments of confusion and resistance—she had not noticed her own word when she uttered it—says, "*Why* don't I want another baby? Any normal woman would! It's not normal!" She is now articulating her feelings—that she thinks she should but does not want to—more clearly and genuinely than she has been able to before. Consider how little the therapist says to produce this effect. Consider how little he has to know about the patient to say what he does say: "Almost?" He has to know, actually, next to nothing.

But if the therapist, in the instance at hand at least (and, I believe, generally in the examples cited throughout this book), does not need deep knowledge of the patient or of the patient's mind in order to communicate something that is therapeutically effective, what is it that enables him to do so? I suggested earlier that the therapist's most fundamental equipment for his work consists simply of his being another person, a person with a point of view different from the patient's. That condition is fundamental, but obviously not sufficient. In this case also, for example, it is easy to imagine the patient's friends reacting to her in quite a different way. One can easily imagine her friends failing to notice the reservation expressed in her "almost," or noticing it dimly and dismissing it, saying nothing in recognition of it. One can, in fact, easily imagine her friends actively encouraging the patient in the conscientious effort she is making to discover a desire in herself to "go ahead." It is easy to imagine this because her friends might easily feel that such support of the patient's own effort was expected of them, and they might wish not to fail that expectation. But if so—if others are limited, or limit themselves, in their response to the patient to what they think is expected of them or to the picture of the patient that the patient herself provides—then we may begin to understand what is different in the therapist's attitude toward the patient. For if the ordinary social tendency is as described, it sacrifices, for social convenience, the therapeutic advantage of an independent view of the patient.

The therapist treats with respect and does not dismiss what he recognizes in the patient, even when it is inconsistent with the picture that the patient intends to present of himself or with the patient's expectation of him. Furthermore, the therapist is willing to talk to the patient about those aspects of the patient that the patient himself does not recognize and may not wish to recognize. These things alone mark the therapist's attitude toward the patient and relationship with him as being of a special kind. This is the communicative attitude that Kaiser speaks of as essential to therapeutic effectiveness.

The patient expects a relationship consistent with the way he sees himself, his circumstances, and his problems. His expectations of the therapeutic relationship and of the therapist's attitude are accordingly limited by his self-deceptions. But the therapist does not feel obliged to respect these limitations, or to humor him by a pretense of doing so. For instance, the patient expects to be treated like a child, perhaps a backward child or, possibly, a precocious child. The therapist talks to him not only like an adult but like an adult who, strangely, expects to be treated like a child. The patient expects to be reformed, "improved," cured of his vices. The therapist has no interest in doing these things and tries only to understand without favoritism, with as much respect for the vices' reasons as for any others. The patient presents his problem from a certain perspective. He tries to dispel his concerns and avoid awareness of them. The therapist feels free to talk not only about that problem but also about the way the patient sees it and presents it, and about its relation to the larger problem of the patient himself. He speaks directly, and without invitation, of the patient's efforts at self-deception and therefore, also of unrecognized concerns. Altogether, the therapist offers a relationship that is more realistic, "straighter," not compromised by deference to the patient's self-deceptions; it is a relationship of greater communicative exchange (although the subject of that exchange is one-sided) and, in that sense, of greater intimacy than ordinary social relationships. The attitude on the part of the therapist that makes that relationship possible is inseparable from the therapist's interest in introducing the patient to himself.

The arrangements of therapy—principally its privacy and continuity—and its mutually accepted professional purposes permit such a therapeutic attitude and relationship. They would certainly be resented as presumptuous elsewhere. But the capacity for such an attitude and relationship is a human capacity and can easily be imagined outside a therapeutic context.

Consider the following comic scene from George Bernard Shaw's play, *Arms and the Man,* written in 1894, and subtitled *An Anti-Romantic Comedy.*

The two characters are Raina, the spoiled daughter of a rich family, conscious of her beauty and given to striking dramatic poses, and Captain Bluntschli, a matter-of-fact, but friendly, Swiss soldier. Raina has just accused Bluntschli of causing her to tell (in order to protect him) the only two lies she has told in her whole life, and she has struck a tragic pose. The stage directions are Shaw's.

BLUNTSCHLI *(dubiously):* You said you'd told only two lies in your whole life. Dear Young Lady, isn't that rather a short allowance? I'm quite a straightforward man myself, but it wouldn't last me a whole morning.

RAINA *(staring haughtily at him):* Do you know, sir, that you are insulting me?

BLUNTSCHLI: I can't help it. When you strike that noble attitude and speak in that thrilling voice, I admire you, but I find it impossible to believe a single thing that you say.

RAINA *(superbly):* Captain Bluntschli!

BLUNTSCHLI *(unmoved):* Yes?

RAINA *(standing over him as if she could not believe her senses):* Do you mean what you said just now? Do you know what you said just now?

BLUNTSCHLI: I do.

RAINA *(gasping):* I! I!! *(She points to herself incredulously, meaning "I, Raina Petkoff, tell lies!" He meets her gaze unflinchingly. She suddenly sits down beside him and adds, with a complete change of manner from the heroic to the familiar)* How did you find me out?

BLUNTSCHLI: Instinct, dear lady. Instinct, and experience of the world.

RAINA *(wonderingly):* Do you know, you are the first man I ever met who did not take me seriously.

BLUNTSCHLI: You mean, don't you, that I am the first man that has ever taken you quite seriously?

RAINA: Yes, I suppose I do mean that. *(At her ease with him)*

How strange it is to be talked to in such a way! You know
I've always gone on like that.
BLUNTSCHLI: You mean the—?
RAINA: I mean the noble attitude and the thrilling voice.
(They laugh together) I did it when I was a tiny child to
my nurse. She believed in it. I do it before my parents.
They believe in it.[4]

Sometimes, therapists speak of their work as depleting. They
usually mean that it continually requires a kind of giving, perhaps of sympathy, encouragement, or support. One author has
indicated that he does not consider that he has done his best
for his patients unless he feels exhausted at the end of the day.
But this view of what is required of the therapist is surely
incorrect. On the contrary, it seems evident that if the therapist finds the therapy hour consistently depleting, something
is wrong: communication is not taking place.

In personal relations in general, a gain for one is also a gain
for the other, not a loss; a satisfactory experience for one is a
satisfactory experience for the other. It is so in psychotherapy
as well. The achievement of contact with a patient who was
previously cut off from himself, and therefore from the therapist, is a satisfying experience for both. The experience of
successful communication with someone, and of achieving successful communication, of talking to and understanding each
other, even if about matters of more intrinsic concern to one
than the other, is an interesting and satisfying experience. It
is true, of course, in psychotherapy that such efforts are very
often unsuccessful, or unsuccessful to some degree, and therefore frustrating, leaving the therapist conscious of his limita-

[4]Bernard Shaw, *Arms and the Man,* in his *Seven Plays* (New York: Dodd, Mead,
1951).

tions or ineptitude. But even then, the experience is not usually exhausting or even especially taxing. Either one succeeds in understanding and in making contact or one fails, in one degree or another, hour by hour. Labor, hard effort will not make the difference.

What is taxing and depleting is the effort to give sympathy when it is not there—to be concerned, to be interested, or to look interested, when one is bored. Talking to someone about something one is interested in is not taxing; neither on the whole is listening to someone talk about something in which he is interested. It is being with someone without contact or genuine communication, listening at length to someone when he himself is not interested in what he is saying or does not believe it, that is taxing and exhausting. And this is especially so when, though not experiencing contact or communication with the patient and, consequently, not genuinely interested, the therapist feels obliged to behave as if he were.

The Traditional Analytic Relationship

In the traditional arrangement for psychoanalysis—the patient lying on a couch, the analyst sitting behind—the analyst cannot see the patient's face to any extent. Certainly he cannot see the patient's expression. The patient's view of the analyst, of course, is more restricted, and the effects of limiting the patient's field are important also, but they are often discussed. Here I wish to consider the significance of the analyst's limited view. It is, one might think, a serious handicap to the aim of empathic listening and understanding. Either that, or it reflects a very special kind of empathic listening and understanding.

The well-known analyst Theodor Reik has remarked that the patient in analysis does not actually talk *to* the analyst; he talks *before* the analyst.[5] This observation is probably somewhat overstated; perhaps Reik should have said that the patient talks before the analyst to the extent that he consciously follows the basic rule. It is largely in connection with that effort that the patient presents his thoughts and "associations" before the analyst without censorship or conscious direction, to the extent that he can.[6]

Correspondingly, in this relationship the analyst must listen in a special way: he must *listen for* psychodynamically significant material in what the patient provides. This kind of listening has often been discussed in the analytic literature. Reik himself speaks of it as "listening with the third ear," by which he means the analyst's attempt to allow himself a special imaginative and associative freedom in listening to the patient's productions, the better to grasp their possible unconscious or metaphorical significance.[7] Although the couch is certainly not essential either to the special kind of talking expected of the patient or to the analyst's special kind of listening, it seems clear that it is no handicap to either one and, if anything, facilitates both. Freud's remark that it was personally more

[5]Theodor Reik, *Listening with the Third Ear* (New York: Farrar, Straus, 1949), p. 108.

[6]It thus seems futile for the analyst to take care, as Freud ("On Beginning the Treatment: Further Recommendations in the Technique of Psychoanalysis" [1913] *Standard Edition*, 12:139 [London: Hogarth Press, 1958]) and, following him, Otto Fenichel (*Problems of Psychoanalytic Technique* [New York: Psychoanalytic Quarterly Press, 1941]), warn he should, that the patient not be allowed to divide the session into an official and an unofficial part, since the patient's doing so merely recognizes the reality of the analytic arrangement. In effect, it is normally expected that the patient will talk briefly *to* the analyst on entering and departing, but talk *before* him while on the couch. The recommendation, if anything, should be that the analyst be aware of the use to which the patient may put this imposed division.

[7]Reik, *Listening with the Third Ear* [5].

comfortable for him to sit out of his patients' sight is often recalled. It is less often noted that Freud went on to say that it was particularly the special kind of listening his work required that made this arrangement more comfortable.[8] It is undoubtedly helpful for the analyst's imaginative and associative freedom, for "listening with the third ear" to the patient's productions, that the analyst allow himself a certain disengagement from the present reality of the patient, from his earnest looks, his expectant glances, his urgent questions, and so forth.

The analyst listens for the unconscious and irrational voice of the patient, but he talks to the conscious, rational patient. A collaborative relationship is assumed to exist between analyst and patient, or at least such a relationship is thought to be necessary for ultimate success. This collaboration—generally emphasized in psychoanalytically derived psychotherapy more than in classical psychoanalysis—is not on the basis of equal responsibility, of course, but on the basis of a "joint effort," as Freud spoke of it, according to their respective roles. The separation—according to the traditional conception of neurotic self-estrangement—of irrational, anachronistic, unconscious aims and fantasies from a more or less rational consciousness implies the possibility of such a joint therapeutic effort to uncover and understand those anachronistic elements in the patient's psychology. I referred earlier (in chapter 3) to the embodiment of such a relationship in the problematical concept of "therapeutic alliance," at least in some of its versions. Thus it is to the presumably rational—or, as it is sometimes called, "contemplative"—ego that the analyst addresses himself when he asks the patient to follow the basic rule, or to which psychotherapists speak when they request the patient to

[8]Freud, "On Beginning the Treatment" [6], p. 133.

talk about his feelings or his problems, or to join the therapist in working on them. It is to this presumed aspect of the patient that the analyst or therapist addresses his interpretations and, at least finally, on which he relies for their acceptance.[9]

In these respects the patient is regarded as being a collaborator with the analyst or therapist; and in this role, insofar as he fulfills it—in being productive, following the basic rule, or talking about his feelings, his problems, and so on—he is therefore outside the scope of immediate therapeutic interest. He is tacitly regarded as the disinterested self-observer and provider of material, not as constituting the material himself. This is the framework of the traditional therapeutic concentration on the text that the patient produces. From this standpoint, it is only when the patient fails in his collaborative role, when he falls silent or is otherwise resistant—as when he is affected by negative transference reactions—that therapeutic interest returns from the material that he provides to him.

In reality, however, when the patient attempts to comply with the basic rule, conscious direction and purpose of speech do not actually cease. His speech simply becomes directed according to his understanding of the requirements of that rule. In fact, it seems likely that the effect on the patient of his effort to comply with the basic rule is generally in the opposite direction from what might be expected: the articulation of thoughts and feelings becomes more, not less, self-conscious than in direct communication. The same applies to the request commonly made to the patient in psychotherapy, more or less corresponding to the basic rule, to talk about his

[9]As I noted earlier, however, Freud's view of the joint effort, out of which the concept of the therapeutic alliance developed, relied not on a "contemplative" component of the ego but—more plausibly—on a conscious component of the positive transference, a rapport with the analyst. See "The Dynamics of the Transference" (1912) *Standard Edition*, 12:105 (London: Hogarth Press, 1958).

problems and his feelings. In both of these cases—though neither the patient nor the therapist may recognize the fact— the patient, to the extent that he is affected at all, is likely to retain a higher level of consciousness of his patientness than otherwise. He becomes more conscious of his role as patient in the "joint effort" and directs himself accordingly. This is often evident, for example, in the prevalence of the self-conscious form of speech: "I feel . . . ," "I think . . . ," "I'm depressed today . . . ," and the like. The speech form is explicitly the form of a report. But the self-conscious attitude need not necessarily be accompanied by this explicit speech form.

Consciousness of the role of patient has many variations, and the particular ways of "talking before" the therapist associated with them have many nuances. I have mentioned before, for example, patients who search without realizing it for something "appropriate" to say.

A patient falls silent for a moment, then remarks, "I have nothing to say."

THERAPIST: Perhaps you mean you have nothing you want to say.
PATIENT: No. It's simply that I have nothing to say, nothing appropriate.
THERAPIST: Appropriate?
PATIENT: Well, problem areas.

For other patients, the patient role and its attendant responsibility of "talking before" the therapist has the general character of an essentially humble or contrite recognition of one's psychological failings or, in a similar spirit, of a dutiful effort at self-improvement or self-reform. Another patient, feeling somewhat better and searching uneasily for something to say, explains that to *talk to* the therapist without "admitting" something or being otherwise mindful of his psychological "shortcomings" seems "arrogant" and "smug." It is, he feels, particularly so because he does after all still have such "short-comings." Still another patient compares the situation in the therapist's office, when the patient has no psychological problems to "discuss"—that is, when he is obliged, for lack of "material," to depart from his collaborative role—with his previous discomfort in meeting the therapist by chance outside the office.

Although the patient's consciousness of his role, with its various ways of talking before the therapist, is fostered by the traditional conception of the collaborative therapeutic relationship, it undoubtedly develops to some extent in all psychotherapy, especially with knowledgeable patients. The assumption of such a role and way of relating does not present any special therapeutic problem if it is recognized and eventually articulated by the therapist. The point is, rather, that a role consciousness and mode of communication of this sort may be unrecognized effects of therapeutic arrangements or instructions that have other aims. What may seem to be simple therapeutic instructions to the patient—say, to talk about his feelings—tacitly define the patient's relation to the therapeutic process, to the therapist, and to himself as a participant. If this role consciousness and particular mode of communication are implicit in the therapeutic arrangements and instruction without the therapist's recognition of the fact, it is entirely possible for exchange to take place indefinitely concerning what the patient has said that will be experienced by the patient according to that role, however it is intended by the therapist. Such an exchange will not result in any new contact with the patient or fresh articulation of his feelings, but only in the satisfaction of that unrecognized role, that is, of doing his therapeutic work. The exchange will have become ceremonial instead of communicative.

There is another, more general effect of this kind of collaborative therapeutic relationship on the patient's communication. It concerns the very success of that relationship in helping patients to talk more freely, more personally, than they would be likely to do otherwise. There is no doubt that a therapeutic relationship in general, a collaborative therapeutic relationship of this sort in particular, and the use of a couch most of all make it easier for most patients to talk about their personal lives than it would be otherwise. But it is well to recognize that such a benefit has a cost.

Why should it be easier to talk to a therapist than, say, to a friend? The reason the couch arrangement makes it easier for most people to talk is, one will think, obvious. For the other person to be out of one's sight, above all not to have to meet his glance, is to feel less ashamed of what one has to say. But therein lies the problem. The experience of shame is diminished for the patient on the couch precisely because the sense of contact, of directness of communication, with another person is diminished. If the experience of telling another person what one feels or thinks and of seeing in the other's eyes that he has understood is diluted—as in talking behind a screen or saying it by mail or even over the telephone rather than face-to-face—then one's own momentary sensation of what one is feeling or thinking is less acute. What dilutes the experience of saying it also dilutes the awareness of feeling it.

It is for this reason that it is not only the special arrangement of the couch that makes it easier for the patient to talk. His consciousness of his role as a patient, including his mode of "talking before" the therapist; his sense of doing his therapeutic work; and his general awareness of therapeutic rules and expectations all make it easier for the patient to talk because they all dilute his sensation of simply saying what he believes, what he feels, and what he has done. The awareness that he is talking *before* the therapist as he is supposed to, that he is providing material, the general sense that he is at the moment being the cooperative patient (who says, "I feel . . . ," "I had the thought . . ."), dilutes his awareness of his feelings. In this way, articulations by the patient that might be expected to sharpen his consciousness of feelings, ideas, or motivations may actually blur that consciousness, or at least sharpen it much less than direct communication would.

I referred in an earlier example to a twenty-four-year-old divorced female patient who reluctantly tells her male therapist that she has had a dream about him. It is very difficult to tell him this dream, she says, or even to mention its existence, because telling it, even telling about it, "amplifies it." There is, however, an addendum to the example. The patient is struggling with the problem when, a few moments later, another thought occurs to her. She remembers that she is, after all, "a patient telling my therapist" a dream. She adds, "That makes it easier."

From a Collaborative Relationship to a Communicative Relationship

I have discussed the close relation between the patient's communicative contact with the therapist on the one hand and the patient's self-awareness, or contact with himself, on the other. I am suggesting now that an aspect of psychoanalytic tradition, inherited by psychotherapy in general, which casts the patient partly in the role of self-observer and provider of material, talking *before* the therapist, limits the directness of that communicative contact and thus continues a partial estrangement of the patient from the very "material" that he provides. As I stated earlier, communication to another person is, at the same time, articulation of oneself. If that is so, it may also be said that diminishing the directness of communication dilutes consciousness of that articulation.

In Freud's early use of hypnosis to gain access to the therapeutic material—at the time consisting of the pathogenic memories—the conscious patient was, in a sense, excluded. Freud abandoned the method, partly for that reason, in favor of the method of free association. In doing so, he made a farsighted trade. He sacrificed the promise of more immediate access to the pathogenic memories for the sake of a greater communication with the patient. Now, a further step, a more complete departure from that earliest practice, is justified. It is true that freer access to the patient's thoughts and feelings is to be gained by assigning the patient a role of the sort I have described in the traditional collaborative relationship. But there is a cost involved that must be included in the calculation of that apparent gain. When that cost in the possibility of directness of communication is considered, it seems reasonable to dispense with arrangements and instructions to the patient that foster talking *before* the therapist and, instead, allow him to talk *to* the therapist as he will and to the extent that he can. The result may well be an initially diminished production of personal information. But the obstacles to communication that are intrinsic to the psychology of the patient will become more visible, and the possibility of achieving communicative contact will be increased.

Chapter 8

The Question of
Historical Interpretation

The therapeutic use of personal history has acquired a peculiar status. On the one hand, there is no doubt that both historical understanding of a certain sort and historical interpretation remain important to psychoanalytically derived therapy in general, as well as to psychoanalysis itself. On the other hand, it is generally accepted that the recovery of early childhood memories is at best extremely incomplete and that what little is recovered is of doubtful reliability. In fact, serious questions about historical reconstruction in general—not only about the nature of its therapeutic function and the extent of its therapeutic value, but about its truth or validity, even its theoretical possibility—have been raised among psychoanalysts themselves. Some have rejected outright as psychologically untenable the idea of passively registered, still preserved, therapeutically unearthed childhood causes of adult psychological

The Question of Historical Interpretation

reactions.[1] They have proposed a more relativistic view of the childhood history that is developed through psychoanalysis, an explicit recognition of it as a subjective, retrospective, and even specifically psychoanalytic construction rather than an unearthing of what has been objectively laid down. They argue that what had been assumed in psychoanalysis to be simple reconstructions of childhood history were actually such constructions all along, starting with Freud's own cases. The argument is very strong and entirely convincing. But it implies, at the very least, that the conception and justification of a continued systematic therapeutic use of historical material would have to be quite different from the original psychoanalytic ones. As Jean Schimek says, "we must face the fact that Freud's explanation and rationale for the process of [historical] interpretation are no longer adequate."[2]

Donald Spence's view on the matter is extreme and frankly pragmatic. The analyst's constructions of personal history are, as he puts it, "means to future effects and not the result of past causes."[3] The analyst constructs a historical picture "in the sincere belief that [it] will facilitate the process of therapy";[4] specifically, that it will enable the patient "to see his life as continuous, coherent and, therefore, meaningful."[5] The pragmatism of Spence's position seems to me incompatible with an

---

[1]See especially Jean G. Schimek, "The Interpretations of the Past: Childhood Trauma, Psychical Reality, and Historical Truth," *Journal of the American Psychoanalytic Association* 23 (1975): 845–65; also, Roy Schafer, *The Analytic Attitude* (New York: Basic Books, 1983), chaps. 12, 13; and Donald Spence, *Narrative Truth and Historical Truth* (New York: W. W. Norton, 1982).

[2]Jean G. Schimek, "Fact and Fantasy in the Seduction Theory: An Historical Review," *Journal of the American Psychoanalytical Association* 35, no. 4 (1987): 937–65.

[3]Spence, *Narrative Truth* [1], p. 274.

[4]Ibid., p. 275.

[5]Ibid., p. 280.

acceptable therapeutic relationship. (What would he say if his patient asked of an interpretation "Do you tell me that because you believe it or because you think it would be good for *me* to believe it?") But even short of this kind of pragmatism, if systematic historical construction is no longer aimed at unearthing a preserved pathogenic past, some justification not far from Spence's of its continued therapeutic use would seem inevitable. If the purpose of systematic historical construction is, indeed, only to provide the patient with a more coherent idea of himself and a more complete and continuous sense of his personal history, then it seems to me that the always questionable didactic elements of its traditional use will have been retained while its original and (at least in principle) far more powerful therapeutic purpose of bringing repressed memories and fantasies into consciousness will have been abandoned. In other words, this new use of historical construction seems likely to provide the patient only with a new role of himself, a new—if presumably more satisfactory or "meaningful"— content for self-consciousness.

Historical or Characterological Understanding?

Let us keep in mind the kind of historical understanding, and therapeutic use of it, being considered here. It is not historical understanding in the usual developmental sense that is in question, not the obvious fact that adults—neurotic and otherwise—have developmental histories. It is specifically the traditional psychoanalytic kind of historical understanding of psychopathology, and it posits a direct effect of early childhood experience, whether actual event or fantasy, unconsciously preserved intact, in adult symptom, reaction, attitude, or relationship.

It was actually Freud's and Breuer's prepsychoanalytic trauma theory of neurosis that contained the most compelling justification for the therapeutic recovery of childhood history. The relation between that conception of the illness and that definition of the therapy was absolutely clear. The neurosis—responsible for the specific symptom, isolated from the personality—was thought to consist of the memory of a childhood event preserved in a special, as if abcessed, condition. "Hysterics suffer from reminiscences" was Freud's formulation. The therapeutic necessity for the recovery of that memory, as directly as possible, through hypnosis, in order to permit the catharsis or abreaction, is obvious and logically inescapable.

But from the time that the concept of an actual trauma is replaced as the presumed pathogenic agent by the concept of developmentally, instinctually, generated wishes and fantasies and their conflicts—that is, from the beginning of psychoanalysis proper—the recovery of pathogenic memories or fantasies was no longer so simple an idea, no longer so directly achievable, and no longer so self-evidently curative. This is especially true after the initial psychoanalytic phase of comparatively direct "symptom analysis." Increasingly, neurosis was recognized as a more complicated matter, far more widespread throughout mental life in symptom and derivative than in its earlier conception.[6] Not only was the recovery of early

[6]Freud himself raised the question in 1926 of whether such symptoms and derivatives were necessarily still dependent for their energy and direction on their original infantile source or might have become independent vehicles of conflict. "Do the old wishes, about whose former existence analysis tells us, still exist? The answer seems ready at hand and certain. It is that the old repressed wishes must still be present in the unconscious since we still find their derivatives, the symptoms, in operation. But this answer is not sufficient. It does not enable us to decide between two possibilities;

memories opposed by resistance but, even when apparently achieved, it was admittedly not necessarily therapeutically effective—hence the necessity of a further phase of "working through." It was, in fact, the great value of the transference concept that it rescued the therapeutic effort from its theoretical reliance on the recovery of early memories and fantasies by its presumed re-creation of their elements in the relationship with the therapist (although, inasmuch as the transference had still in principle to be retranslated into recovered memory, the theoretical rescue was only partial).

From a clinical standpoint, with the recognition of the characterological nature of neurosis, the concept of the unconsciously preserved and dynamically effective infantile experience becomes untenable. It becomes untenable for exactly the reasons the concept of the preserved nuclear infantile conflict becomes untenable; the two are virtually synonymous. In assuming the direct effect of early experience on adult behavior, reaction, or relationship, they fail to recognize and circumvent the existence of adult personality and the attitudes of adult consciousness. Indeed, they circumvent or "short-circuit" the intervening developmental process.[7] That is the objection in its general form. Specifically, the form of the relevant infantile experience cannot possibly encompass the forms of the adult symptomatology, traits, and behavior that it is presumed to explain, not to speak of the adult neurotic character as a whole. Indeed, the effort to encompass adult symptoms and behavior

---

either that the old wish is now operating only through its derivatives, having transferred the whole of its cathectic energy to them, or that it is itself still in existence too. . . . There are many things about mental life, both normal and pathological, which seem to call for the raising of such questions" (*Inhibitions, Symptoms and Anxiety* [1926], *Standard Edition*, 20:142 [London: Hogarth Press, 1959]).

[7]See Schimek, "Interpretations of the Past" [1], p. 860.

within prototypes in infantile experience has led to the objection that it retrospectively endows the young child with adult mental capacities. It is this last objection that led Jean Piaget, generally respectful of psychoanalysis, to complain that it was "not developmental enough"[8] and "too much a science of the permanent."[9]

But it is not only that the early prototypes cannot encompass the adult symptomatology. Above all, from a clinical standpoint, the idea of the preserved infantile experience, cut off from the developing personality, as a direct cause of adult symptomatology is refuted by the fact that that symptomatology is invariably consistent with, and not an intrusion into, adult character and attitudes. And it is not only symptomatology in the general sense in which I have described it that is consistent with adult character and attitudes, but also specific reactions and specific kinds of relationships—such as transference reactions and relationships—that can be shown to derive from adult character and attitudes.

Once again, it is well to remember that the concept of dissociated infantile experience, preserved intact, was originally intended to explain a picture of neurotic symptoms as isolated intrusions into the rational adult personality. It was that picture of the isolated symptom which gave the concept its explanatory power. And even though they are no longer seen as isolated from the personality, the existence of all sorts of subjectively estranged or partially estranged symptoms and reactions ("What do I see in him!", "I want to stop drinking, but I can't," etc.) in the various neurotic conditions continues to

[8]Jean Piaget, *Intelligence and Affectivity: Their Relationship During Child Devel opment*, trans. and ed. T. A. Brown and C. E. Kaegi (Palo Alto, Calif.: Annual Reviews, 1981), p. 37.

[9]Jean Piaget, *Play Dreams and Imitation in Childhood*, trans. C. Gattegno and F. M. Hodgson (New York: W. W. Norton, 1962), p. 186.

give plausibility to that conception, even apparently to require it. The reaction or symptom that is strange to the rational adult mind is assumed to have its source elsewhere. Where else, if not in some still-preserved piece of the past? But once we look closely at neurotic personality, another sort of explanation becomes possible. It becomes apparent that there are schisms in that personality of a different kind and dynamics of a different kind than have been thought. It becomes apparent that the neurotic personality reacts against itself, with the consequence that the neurotic person does not know himself. It is not a case, as it once seemed, of a rational adult being affected by an estranged voice of his childhood. It is, rather, a case of an adult who does not recognize his own adult voice. It is a case of an adult who so deceives himself that he thinks he is, feels he must be, more manly or more honorable than he is; who thinks he hates someone or that he feels self-confident when he does not; who is not merely out of touch with particular memories or fantasies but is unaware of whole aspects of his subjective experience. The case is in a way more peculiar than was thought; the self-deception, the distortion of self-awareness in a way is greater.

This view of neurotic self-estrangement allows a more complete understanding of neurotic symptomatology than the assumption of preserved infantile experience because it allows explanation of adult symptomatology and reaction as effects of unrecognized and unarticulated adult attitudes, subjective experience, and subjective dynamics. In other words, it allows explanation of adult symptomatology in terms of the dynamics and the nature of the adult personality. It thus becomes the articulation of the workings of that personality, rather than the recovery of preserved infantile experience, that is therapeutically essential.

Such a picture of neurotic personality does not deny the

existence of childhood conflict or its developmental influence. It asserts, however, that the lasting significance of such conflict resides in its *effect on development* rather than its *separation from development*. Childhood conflict is not preserved intact, but it may distort development in ways that are not easily reversed. Memories derived from childhood conflict and anxiety may still be powerfully affecting; not because their original intensity has been preserved by isolation but, on the contrary, because they have been sustained by their developmental significance or have been reconstructed according to their contemporary significance.

The Source of Anxiety

Consider the understanding of neurotic anxiety in terms of preserved infantile conflict. Anxiety, it is thought, must ultimately be derived from the expectation of danger. Hence, where there is no actual present danger, even, as it seems, from the subject's own conscious standpoint, anxiety must be derived from the unconsciously preserved anticipation of some, most likely fantasied, childhood danger. The fantasied dangers of childhood made most familiar by psychoanalysis are the danger of the child's helpless abandonment, the danger of castration, and the danger of punishment by the superego (behind which ultimately stands the parental threat). Thus in this view, aims, intentions, or circumstances that are derivatives, displacements, or representations of childhood prototypes arouse an anticipatory anxiety signal of the childhood threat which, in turn, triggers various inhibitory or defensive reactions.

Freud said, "The adult's ego . . . continues to defend itself against dangers which no longer exist."[10] How else can one account for neurotic anxiety and inhibition in reaction to some apparently innocuous intention or behavior or circumstance? What else could the threat consist of, if not some representation of a past danger that the present stands for or calls up? But a different answer—in a sense a different *type* of answer—is possible. A particular feeling, intention, or action can acquire a threatening significance not from a rearousal of infantile expectations of dangerous external consequences, but from the nature of the internal experience of it; from the quality of its subjective experience *by an individual of a particular personality*, especially when that experience is not recognized or consciously articulated.

Feelings, motivations, and intentions have their existence in individuals of particular personalities, and they must be understood subjectively. But the tradition of psychological theory, including psychoanalytic theory, has been to consider motivations abstractly and nonsubjectively as drives, needs, or directed energies of one sort or another. Even when the subjectivity of motivation is recognized in principle—as when it is treated as wish—it is usually without reference to the particular person or kind of person whose subjective experience it is.

If feelings, motivations, or actions are considered in an abstract way, more or less as vectors detached from the personality in which they actually have their existence, it is true that they can only be imagined to give rise to anxiety or inhibition through their association with some real or imagined external danger or punishment. If an abstract internal force gives rise to anxiety, one can only imagine its association with some sort of external danger. There is no other variable, no other agency,

[10]Sigmund Freud, "Analysis Terminable and Interminable" (1937) *Standard Edition*, 23:238 (London: Hogarth Press, 1964).

in the picture. But when we speak of motivations or intentions or actions as they are experienced by an individual of a particular personality, that picture changes. We then imply the existence of a subjective point of view, of particular forms or qualities of subjective experience, of specific kinds and thresholds of tolerance and of ways of reaction to the awareness of ideas or sensations that exceed those thresholds. Some kinds of feelings or motivations, as they approach conscious articulation and self-awareness, will be congenial to a particular individual's attitudes and sense of self. Others will be intolerable, and their sensation—or the individual's incipient awareness of them—will trigger various kinds of anxious discomfort and various kinds of inhibiting and consciousness-distorting processes, according to the nature of his personality. I have described and illustrated these dynamics of subjective experience before.

This understanding is only consistent with common experience. We know and can predict that a certain person will not, cannot, do a certain thing. It is quite possible that we can make that prediction entirely without knowledge of his childhood or his personal history. Our knowledge and our prediction is based on our knowledge of *him,* that is, his makeup, his attitudes and feelings. Knowledge of his childhood history is not only unnecessary but would in fact help us very little once we know him. We know that he would find a certain act intolerable and that any thought of committing it would be abhorrent. He cannot be imagined to do it; or rather, he cannot be imagined as choosing or being willing to do it. (For it is not the doing, as in a drugged or intoxicated state, or inadvertently or, in some cases, under external compulsion that is unimaginable, but the feeling and the attitude that such a willingness or intention implies.) And if we think that we have succeeded in imagining him doing it, we realize quickly that we are not imagining him at all, but someone else.

That is instructive. If we cannot imagine a certain individual we know—a person of certain feelings and attitudes—choosing to do something that might easily be imaginable for someone else, we can perhaps more easily understand the significance of his abhorrence of it and the nature of his anxiety. If it is true that to do, or to choose to do, a certain thing one would have to be a different person with quite different feelings and attitudes, then the incipient awareness of the wish or intention to do that thing must threaten the sense of oneself as one is. Is that not what patients express in the quality of their anxiety at the idea of some action which we know to be inimical to their general attitudes and sense of themselves? A rigidly dutiful person is offered a better job but says he would feel "irresponsible," "running away from a challenge," if he left his present onerous one "just because" he wants to. A timid person says she feels "brazen" telling the therapist that she notices he has gotten new glasses. Are these people not saying that the attitudes contained in such actions, the experience of themselves deliberately doing these things, threatens their present sense of themselves in specific ways? And are they not right to perceive such a threat? From this standpoint, we must say that Freud was wrong when he assumed that apparently innocuous motivations that give rise to anxiety must raise the spectre of dangers that "no longer exist."

It is true that this understanding of anxiety can, with some justification, be called circular. The rigid person experiences anxiety when he is about to make a personal choice. Why? Because he is a rigid person. The answer admittedly does not offer the satisfaction of a direct relation to an original cause in the form of an external danger or the imagination of one. But it is a realistic answer. Human personality is more densely organized than psychoanalysis, even in its elaboration of the ego, has so far conceived it to be. It is far less a mere transmitter or simple template of its own early history than was thought.

In my opinion we do not know very much as yet about the origins and development of neurosis; but let us assume that the experience of anxiety *was* originally in reaction to the expectation of real or imagined danger. Assume further that the experience of such anxiety tends to promote, in the child's personality, the development of restrictive attitudes—such as a rigid consciousness of rules or timid attitudes—which forestall, at least in most circumstances, that experience of anxiety. (Here I am saying no more than that the development of the personality probably bears some resemblance, in its adaptive principles, to its later anxiety-dispelling or anxiety-forestalling dynamics.) As such restrictive attitudes come into existence, then, the further awareness of certain motivations and feelings will be inimical to them, will arouse anxiety, and will trigger some sort of inhibitory or corrective reaction according to those attitudes. The subjective experiences that are *now* inimical to those restrictive attitudes need not be identical to the ones that were originally experienced as dangerous. The nature of the tendencies and the circumstances that will be inimical to the restrictive personality will be determined by the nature of that restrictiveness, not by the experiences that originally contributed to its development. The already timid older child or adult will shrink, not merely from the experiences that originally contributed to his timidity, but from much broader categories of experience because he is now a different person. He was then only a *frightened* person; he is now a *timid* person. His timidity will now cause all sorts of objectively innocuous behavior to feel audacious. Thus restrictive attitudes, originally formed in reaction to certain specific anxieties, will in turn transform and greatly enlarge the category of what is anxiety-arousing to include all that is threatening to *them*. In such a way, neurotic personality becomes independent, in its dynamics, of its original sources.

This kind of thinking is not new to psychoanalysis. Some such theoretical recognition of the dynamics of personality is implied in its theory of the ego, again in its theory of the superego, and in general in its recognition of psychological structure, if that is taken to mean a structure of the personality. What else does psychological structure imply if not that certain reactions—for instance inhibiting reactions—which have originally developed in response to particular circumstances may then become reaction tendencies of the personality, assimilated by the personality and at the same time changing it? And, further, does it not imply that these reaction tendencies of the personality may then be independent of the particular circumstances, or even of any associative representation of those circumstances, that were their original stimulus? In this theoretical development, psychoanalysis moved in a new direction but did not leave the old completely behind. At least, this is true to the extent that the ego or superego is not understood to be a thoroughly integrated aspect of the personality but merely a repository for preserved and dynamically still effective memories or fantasies of external inhibiting agents, for internalizations, introjections, identifications, and so forth with independent dynamic effects. Thus I consider the ideas I have set forth here to be a reasonable extension of psychoanalytic theoretical ideas themselves.

The Concept of Transference

From the standpoint of therapy, there is no more important historical concept than that of transference, in its specific meaning of an unconsciously preserved childhood image or fantasy directly transferred to the figure of the therapist. Nor is there a clearer instance of the kind of historical understanding of a specific reaction that slights the significance of the patient's contemporary personality. The adult personality of the patient counts for very little in the traditional conception of the transference reaction beyond an agency of transmission of the preserved past.

The clinical reactions to which that concept refers are not in question. Neither is the developmental significance of the child's early relationships, including the effects of those relationships of which the adult is not conscious. The question is as before whether that significance includes a more or less direct transfer of the childhood prototype to the adult's relationships, particularly the relationship with the therapist. As opposed to that possibility, there is the less simple one that those relationships express no such transfer of importance but, rather, express the dynamics of the adult personality whose development has intervened.

Much the same issues arise in connection with transference as with other symptomatic behavior or reactions. The feelings contained in the transference reaction—or, strictly speaking, the unconscious component of the transference reaction—are considered to have been separated from the developing personality ("held up in the course of development, it has been kept away from the conscious personality")[11] and to be anachronis-

---

[11]Sigmund Freud, "The Dynamics of the Transference" (1912), *Standard Edition*, 12:100 (London: Hogarth Press, 1958).

tic intrusions, preserved more or less intact from the past. But the clinical evidence clearly opposes this view; it shows that these feelings are actually consistent with the general form and the dynamics of adult personality, allowing, of course, for the special conditions of the situation.

For example, it is the rigidly principled defensive young woman, extremely sensitive to indignity at others' hands, but haughty and largely unaware of her own sense of inferiority, who becomes angry with the therapist for his "coldness" and, from the beginning, suspects that he wants to get rid of her. By the same token, it is the exaggeratedly naïve, girlish, suggestible woman who very quickly develops an awed and romantic attachment to the therapist, especially the male therapist.

I have already indicated in chapter 5 that it is possible to derive various "transference" distortions of the therapeutic relationship from the dynamics of the particular neurotic personality, in these special circumstances, without any reference to childhood history at all. In this connection, also, it is probable that infantile prototypes are insufficient to encompass the various forms of adult reaction. In other words, it is likely that freeing the concept of transference reactions from the comparatively limited repertoire of prototypes of early family experience that seems to be available would permit more subtle clinical observations of those reactions.

The patient's distortion of the therapeutic relationship may very well resemble important childhood relationships in various respects. His personality, after all, will have been largely shaped in the course of certain relationships, its ways affected by their possibilities and requirements. These facts are not brought into question by the recognition that the distortions of the adult relationship are creations of the adult personality rather than a direct transference of a preserved childhood memory or fantasy. Specific vestiges and memories—perhaps affecting ones— of childhood relationships remain; but it is their continuing significance to the adult that sustains and energizes them, rather than the other way around.

The issue can be made sharper with an example. An interesting and well-documented one offers itself in the aforementioned case of Schreber,[12] which Freud used in formulating his theory of paranoia as a defense against unconscious homosexual wishes.[13] Comparison of Schreber's delusional ideas about his physician, Dr. Flechsig, and later about God, with documentation of his father's extraordinary character, attitudes, and child-rearing methods makes it clear that an assumption of a psychotic transference could hardly be more justified.[14]

Schreber's primary delusion was that he was being transformed—against his will and to his horror—into a woman, initially by his psychiatrist, Flechsig, and later by God, for purposes of sexual abuse. Freud concluded that the figure who became Schreber's persecutor in the paranoid delusion, Flechsig, was the very one to whom Schreber unconsciously wished to surrender sexually. There can hardly be any doubt about the justification of Freud's idea. Both Schreber's initial horror of such a "demanning" and his "voluptuous" sensation of it are amply documented in the *Memoirs*.

Schreber's father was a zealous reformer (exhorting against the "softness" and "decadence" of society), a physical culture advocate, and an authority on child rearing, as well as an orthopedic physician; and his views were published and widely

<hr />

[12]See Daniel Paul Schreber, *Memoirs of My Nervous Illness*, trans. Ida MacAlpine and Richard A. Hunter (London: William Dawson, 1955).

[13]Sigmund Freud, "Psychoanalytic Notes on an Autobiographical Account of a Case of Paranoia" (1911) *Standard Edition*, 12:9–82 (London: Hogarth Press, 1958).

[14]See William G. Niederland, *The Schreber Case: Psychoanalytic Profile of a Paranoid Personality* (New York: Quadrangle, 1974).

known. He advocated and presumably subjected his own children to an extraordinary regimen of psychological and physical coercion and restraint in accordance with his theories of physical and mental health, upright posture and upright character. Belts, straps, and steel braces of various sorts were combined with "minute and inflexible" rules and prescriptions covering the child's total behavior.[15] The explicit aim of this sadistic discipline was to break the child's will and suppress his "crude nature."

It cannot be doubted that Schreber's delusional ideas about Flechsig's and God's coercion of him contained "vestiges of his concrete life experiences" in the family home, as William Niederland has pointed out.[16] They certainly may have included fantasies, as well as specific sensations, that originated in his early relationship with his Godlike father.[17] It is perhaps only supposition that Schreber's sensations of female sexual "voluptuousness" were initially aroused in response to his father's sadistic regimen and were first directed toward his father; but such suppositions, particularly the first, are hardly implausible. Neither is it possible to doubt that these homosexual wishes and sensations were unrecognized by Schreber as such before his psychosis; indeed, even then they were unrecognized by him as *his*. What, then, considering its evident explanatory power, is unsatisfactory about the hypothesis of direct transference? What is missing?

The problem, once again, is that this understanding circumvents Schreber's adult personality and its dynamics. In that sense, it is not a picture of historical development but a simplification of development; and this simplification involves a

[15]Ibid., p. 56.
[16]Ibid., p. 103.
[17]Ibid., pt. II.

significant sacrifice of understanding. As I indicated earlier, Robert P. Knight, while speaking of Freud's theory of paranoia as among the most widely confirmed ideas of psychoanalysis, nevertheless pointed out, "It does not explain why the paranoiac developed such an intense homosexual wish fantasy, nor why he must deny it so desperately."[18] Freud himself acknowledged that his theory did not account for the particular paranoid form of defense against these abhorrent homosexual wishes.[19] These questions are among the ones that can only be answered by an understanding of Schreber's *personality*. They are questions, therefore, that the direct transference theory will inevitably fail to touch.

Even the sketchy picture of Schreber's personality that emerges from the *Memoirs* does suggest some answers to these questions. It is a picture of a severely rigid and moralistic character ("morally unblemished" was Schreber's own description of himself): dutiful, ascetic, pedantic, and much concerned with dignity and "manly honor," willpower and self-control.[20] There is ample evidence in the *Memoirs* that Schreber believed that he indeed embodied those supposed male virtues. There is also ample evidence that for Schreber this image of manliness, with which he identified himself, stood in every respect at the opposite pole from an image of femaleness as weak, soft, morally debased, sexually wanton and ready for sexual surrender, and suffused with a "voluptuous" eroticism. The polar images are complementary; they reflect a conception of maleness and femaleness from a single point of view and, in more moderate form, they can still be found

[18]Robert P. Knight, "The Relationship of Latent Homosexuality to the Mechanism of Paranoid Delusions," *Bulletin of the Menninger Clinic* 4 (1940): 149–59.

[19]Freud, "Psychoanalytic Notes" [13].

[20]See my *Autonomy and Rigid Character* (New York: Basic Books, 1981), pp. 146ff.

among exaggeratedly manly men. For a rigid man of these attitudes, the image of sexual surrender, specifically, is an especially erotic one, precisely because it is an image of surrender of control, of the rigid and constricting will. Giving in to the coercion of the other one is, at the same time, a subjective experience of relinquishing self-control, one of giving in to the self. And the more "manly" that rigid and moralistic will and self-control are conceived as being, the more likely it is that the image of sexual surrender will be female. Thus, the questions raised before—why should fantasies of female sexual surrender be so abhorrent to a man of this makeup? and, why should such fantasies, at the same time, be so compelling?—turn out to have the same answer. The idea of female sexual surrender is, *to an individual of this character and these attitudes,* an image of unrestrained and abandoned eroticism, in Schreber's words the "voluptuousness" of the "female harlot."

In someone less rigid and less estranged from his own feelings, this internal conflict might have taken the conscious form of a highly ambivalent *internal struggle of will,* a struggle against giving in to the self. In Schreber's case, it was transformed into an ambivalent *defensive* (that is, paranoid) *struggle of will* against surrender to an external coercive figure, his physician. A paranoid development from an extremely rigid, primarily compulsive character has a certain logic; its key is the further intensified rigidity, hence greater instability and defensiveness, of such a character under stress. That the forceful and authoritative Dr. Flechsig, to whom Schreber had already grudgingly submitted as a patient, should be at the same time both the persecutor (the one who attempts to coerce, humiliate, and destroy the will to resist) and the object of sexual surrender follows from the rigid character's ambivalence to the idea of such a surrender.

184

The Question of Historical Interpretation

Certainly it is more than likely that Schreber learned directly from his relationship with his despotic father not only to despise weakness and surrender but also to know their satisfactions. It is also possible, though less likely, that the childhood experience of coerced submission to his father offered itself specifically as an erotic model only later and retrospectively. In any case, it is certain that this relationship was a major determinant in the development of the rigid character and attitudes I have described. *The person he became* was the most important lasting effect of Schreber's childhood relationship with his father. Once he had become that person, the erotic fantasies that were at the same time fascinating and abhorrent to him were no longer dependent for their general form upon the memory of his father. Those fantasies surely used experiences from the past, but they were imaginative products of his adult character—as was his indignant and defensive rejection of them. All these were products of the subjective world of the rigid and "manly" character and its dynamics.

Historical Interpretation

Historical interpretation of the childhood experience as the direct, effective cause of the adult reaction handicaps psychotherapy in two ways. For the therapist, the preoccupation with historical prototypes is a distraction from the subjective world of the patient sitting before him. And for the patient, historical constructions are likely to dilute, rather than enhance, effective therapeutic communication in specific ways.

The first point needs only a brief consideration. The comparative ease with which historical prototypes of a particular reaction can be discovered retrospectively when they are sought (which accounts for the multiplicity of schools favoring one developmental prototype or another) distracts the therapist from further interest in the more complicated dynamics of the patient's present subjective experience. In other words, it offers the therapist—and therefore in turn the patient—an explanatory shortcut.

It is the direct effects of that shortcut on the patient that I wish mainly to consider here. In particular, I want to emphasize that a psychological interpretation that circumvents the personality by the assumption that the present reaction is a direct effect of the preserved past is not complementary to one that respects the dynamics of present subjective experience. The two kinds of understanding will lead the patient in different directions.

I will try to illustrate the point rather schematically. The therapist who communicates, "You resent me because you confuse me with your despotic father, who so often humiliated you," offers a different kind of understanding and a different direction of interest from the therapist who communicates, "You resent me because your pride is so sensitive, your respect for yourself so tentative, that merely to come here as a patient is humiliating."

The latter understanding sees the logic of the patient's reaction in the dynamics of his present, largely unarticulated, subjective world, and it aims to introduce him to that subjective world. The former understanding sees the logic of the patient's reaction in its appropriateness to the child's situation that "no longer exists," and it aims to introduce the patient to that situation. If it is indeed correct that the adult's reaction is responsive to circumstances that "no longer exist," then clearly an interpretation to that effect is necessary to restore the personality's integrity and the patient's sense of that reaction as his own. But if this proposition is incorrect, then the historical interpretation will have exactly the opposite effect. If, in other words, the patient resents the therapist because, unknowingly, he confuses him with his despotic father, then only an awareness of the real identity of the object of his feeling can dissolve it. If, however, the emotional source of his reaction is to be found not directly in the child's still preserved reaction but in the adult's unrecognized attitudes and whole subjective world, then this historical interpretation obscures that fact. For in that case, just when interest in the symptomatic reaction should lead further, deeper into that unarticulated adult subjective world, it is described as a vestige of another world and its relation to the adult world is discredited; the patient is told that he is confusing the present with the past.

If my reasoning has been right, it is not the case that the patient mistakenly identifies as a present danger (or present loss, present figure, etc.) one that no longer exists. Instead, the present actually contains an internal danger for him—not for *any* adult, but for *him*. It is not the case that Schreber, for example, feels a terrifying threat to his manly will because he mistakes Flechsig for the tyrant of his childhood, his father. It is rather that he creates the present external enemy, Flechsig, out of the terrifying sensation of the actual weakness and vulnerability of his manly will—that is, out of the unarticulated sensation of his actual susceptibility to an abhorrent temptation. If this is so, a historical interpretation does not merely offer too "intellectual" an understanding, as such interpretations are sometimes considered to do, but points the patient's attention in the wrong direction. By pointing to circumstances that no longer exist, it implies that his reaction is aberrant to him precisely when we wish to introduce the patient to the fact that it is a reaction intrinsic to him. We wish to introduce him to the fact that *he reacts as he does because he is what he is.*

We make precisely this point when the patient himself suggests some such historical explanation of his own reactions or behavior. For example, when the alcoholic patient says "Something *infantile in me* wants to drink, But *I* don't want to!" the therapist may reasonably answer, in one way or another, "No, I disagree. I think it is you who wants to drink, even though you feel so contemptuous of such an interest that you cannot stand to think that it is you." Or when the patient, referring to her relentless nagging of herself ("He's no good for me! Why do I see him!") says "That's my mother talking! I can hear her saying that to me!" the therapist is likely to point out, "No, that's you saying that to you. Perhaps it was her attitude. But if it was, you must have come to share it, even if you didn't notice that you did. That attitude 'took,' out of all the things she said that didn't take."

It has been said that an interpretation that offers no historical explanation constitutes a reproach.[21] It is not difficult to see the point and the justification of this remark. In civilized society, after all, psychoanalysis won the battle against moralism in regard to mental illness on the basis of historical understanding. This kind of historical explanation is intrinsically exculpatory. It is worth considering why.

I believe there are two reasons. The first is simple: historical explanation is *explanation.* Whether correct or incorrect in particulars, it is scientific and deterministic; and by treating behavior or reaction as having causes and being psychologically understandable it makes moral evaluation seem irrelevant. But there is a second, more problematic factor involved. Historical

[21] I believe it was said by Otto Fenichel, though I have been unable to locate the reference.

explanation of the sort we have been considering is exculpatory not only because it is explanation, but also because it is historical in this particular way. It is exculpatory because, by circumventing the adult personality, it diminishes the adult person's responsibility. It removes the onus of the symptomatic act by diminishing adult authorship of it. It is a humane view of the neurotic person. But its exculpation is too complete to be realistic.

A picture of neurotic personality, with the subjective understanding it implies, offers a more realistic understanding of symptomatic action and a more realistic alternative to moral reproach. Its premise is that the person behaves and reacts according to the way he sees things, whether he is aware of how he sees things or not. According to how one sees things—that is, according to what one is—a particular action will or will not seem the next thing to do. Of course, one's history is a determinant of how one sees things and what one is. But it is not a *direct* determinant of what one does or how one reacts.

This is not to say that historical material has no place in psychotherapy, only that it has no privileged place. Sometimes it is convenient to articulate some aspect of the patient's present subjective world—an attitude or feeling—in a historical way, by reference to some familiar source of it or some turning point in its development. Such a use of history does not suggest that the present reaction is a direct expression of a preserved past. It is merely a way of delineating sharply some feature of the present by reference to the way it, or the patient, came to be so. Apart from that use of personal history, historical material produced by the patient spontaneously has as much place in psychotherapy as any other subject matter—no less, no more. Patients often talk about their childhood spontaneously. When they do, they do so—as about anything else—for present reasons, with present attitudes, interests, and aims.

Sometimes a patient recalls an experience of childhood spontaneously and simply wishes to express and communicate it, perhaps finding it possible to articulate some aspect of it for the first time. This is most likely to occur as a *result* of some therapeutic change—a result, in other words, of arriving at a different point of view that allows a new awareness of old feelings. Sometimes, as with other material, the patient tells of his childhood not so much to communicate an experience to someone else as to dispel a present feeling about it in himself. Thus, an experience is told to prove something, to justify something, to deny something, to admit something. Perhaps the patient tells the story of his early mistreatment by his mother in an effort to justify his treatment of her; or he tells it differently, as if to remind himself that by all rights he should hate her; or he tells it as if he would like to make peace with her but is afraid of being "too soft"; or he tells it like an oft-told legend in which he is not much interested, but expects that the therapist will be. With historical material, as with other material, the therapist is in a position to have a wider view of the significance of what the patient says, the events he recounts, than is the patient himself. The therapist can see, in how the patient talks about events of the past, a present significance that the patient cannot recognize. The patient tells a piece of history: "I always had to show them I wasn't just a mama's boy." He tells it as history; but the therapist realizes, from the way he tells it, that he still feels that way. Or the therapist may introduce the patient, momentarily absorbed in some event of the past, to some feeling or attitude of that time, still unrecognized by the patient but evident in the telling now, and therefore obviously expressive of the present.

The Question of Historical Interpretation

For example, a young doctor, usually appearing to be reserved and imperturbable in his therapy hours, seems in one hour to be struggling to avoid crying. Finally, in response to the therapist's mention of that fact, he does cry. Afterward, in an affecting and genuine way, though still reserved, he tells of having been punished as a child with beatings by his uncle, a police officer who raised him, for commonplace childish failings. The punishments continued, he says, until on one occasion, when a little older, he determined that, no matter what, he would not cry:

PATIENT *(with some pride and satisfaction)*: . . . and I didn't. And that was the last time he ever tried to beat me. . . . I think he got a new respect for me then.
THERAPIST: I think he wasn't the only one—you, also—who got a new respect for you then.

In such an exchange, the aim is neither a reconstruction of the past nor a recovery of it for its own sake. It is no different from the therapeutic aim in general, to bring the patient into contact with one or another aspect of his subjective life.

Chapter 9

The Course of

Therapeutic Change

I believe that most therapists, early in their work, are confronted by a discouraging fact. They discover that it is one thing to bring about a momentary change in a patient, even a strikingly therapeutic change, in which the patient experiences a marked sense of relief and a new sense of what he feels and what he wants to do; but it is quite another thing to make such a change stable and lasting and to build upon it. The one is often comparatively easy to achieve; it can sometimes be accomplished in the course of an hour. The other is exceedingly difficult. It may take years; its progress is certain to be irregular and full of reverses; and even after transient improvement, it may fail altogether. Why should this be so? Why, if striking change can be effected so quickly, should it so often be impermanent? Why should so much further effort be required to stabilize it?

The Course of Therapeutic Change

The facts suggest an unexpected answer: namely, that there are two distinct processes involved in therapeutic change. The first of these processes is the one we have considered already: it consists of the polarization of subject and object that occurs when the patient experiences a new contact with himself, when he achieves a new and clearer conscious articulation of his feelings and aims. This effect is immediate. The second process, which is initiated at the same time, is the effect of this new articulation and change on *attitudes*.

It is not so remarkable that there should be this duality. Every newly articulated feeling and newly focused aim is, at the same time, an embodiment of a changed attitude. Every newly articulated feeling or newly focused aim challenges the existing attitudes that constitute the personality. The first process is immediate, to whatever extent it occurs at all. It is satisfying and relieving, perhaps even exciting. The second process, the stretching and changing of attitudes, is anxious and uncomfortable and by its nature very slow. Attitudes—not to say the organization of attitudes that make up the neurotic personality—are resistant to change. The overall process of therapeutic change that we see is the combined effect of these two processes and has its own dynamics. It is this combined effect that gives the impression of a kind of elasticity of the overall process.

Resistance to Change

Psychotherapy is undoubtedly—and unavoidably—repetitious. It is true that it does not usually feel tedious (and that is probably responsible for the subjective foreshortening of its duration); if it goes well, it is also full of surprises and variety. But this does not alter the fact that in general ways it is repetitious. We introduce a patient to himself, to a feeling or an interest of his, in some particular connection. We see a change in him; he feels a change in himself. His awareness of the nature and object of his interest is sharpened and enlarged. Yet, a week or two later, he may talk about the same thing or about something closely related to it in much the same way as he did originally, as if the new awareness has left him. Why should the same territory have to be won again and again?

An obvious possibility suggests itself. Perhaps it is simply a matter of the usual self-awareness-restricting dynamics of the neurotic personality. The enlargement of self-awareness, inimical to the existing attitudes, excites an experience of anxiety in one form or another. That anxiety in turn triggers a "corrective reaction," which restricts self-awareness. But there is something wrong with this explanation. If our understanding is correct, the dynamics of such corrective reactions depend on their quasi-reflexive operation, outside of conscious awareness. Self-awareness, once achieved, we have thought, deprives those restrictive dynamics of their automatic engagement and their force. This, after all, is the essential therapeutic basis of raising consciousness. When we intervene and articulate what the patient himself cannot spontaneously articulate—when we act in that way to enlarge his self-awareness—we penetrate the otherwise reflexively triggered limits of the restrictive system, and in doing so we—theoretically—disable it. And indeed it seems we do, momentarily. Yet not a week later.

Consider a therapeutic event: An obsessively conscientious teacher talks rather wistfully about the weekend just past. It has been filled with family responsibilities, especially in connection with his two young children. In general, he seems to enjoy the children, but, it turns out, he feels that it is necessary to spend every free moment at home engaged in some way with them, to the exclusion of other interests. Why? "For the sake of their development." As he talks further, it is apparent that, having heard of such a theory, he has become obsessively concerned that he might not be "doing enough." The patient soon realizes that he spends his time as he does not so much for his children's sake as to dispel such nagging concerns about himself. As the hour goes on and this concern with not doing enough is further articulated, he becomes visibly more relaxed. He is obviously particularly attracted by the idea of reclaiming some time for himself. At a certain point, however, his concern returns abruptly, though in a somewhat different form. He says, "But if I just do what I want, I might become totally selfish and inconsiderate!"

Something has occurred between the patient's initially relieving recognition of the essentially ritualistic significance of his behavior and the later abrupt return of his anxiety. It was the continued enlargement of his self-awareness, of his consciousness of his own feelings and interests, and especially his sensation of a quite different attitude from his dutiful one. It was as though he realized suddenly that he had bought a much larger (and much more uncomfortable) package than he had at first thought ("But if I just do what I want . . . !"). There was an almost palpable anxious realization, from the standpoint of his dutiful attitudes, that his new view of his situation, and his anticipations in regard to it, involved a change not only in this particular matter of his life but also in him (". . . I might become totally selfish and inconsiderate").

The subjective developments of those few moments contain at least a general answer to the problem of why a newly articulated feeling, a changed reaction, so often fades from awareness. Therapeutic change can only be brought about in small steps, in particular reactions. But each particular change also embodies an increment of more general change in the person and his attitudes. This fact, the general effect of particular changes, works both in favor of therapeutic aims and against them. On the one hand, it has the consequence that particular symptoms or symptomatic reactions may change or disappear in psychotherapy without ever having been explicitly considered. On the other hand, it means that every particular change arouses a more general threat. A particular anxiety or conflict may have been articulated and a particular feeling or wish, previously unwelcome and unrecognized, may have passed the barrier to self-awareness. But the attitudes embodied in that conflict—with their roots in the dispositions of the personality and their various related feelings, supportive reactions, ideas, and corroborative viewpoints—may still be largely unarticulated. The particular conflict, now consciously articulated, is momentarily resolved; the general attitudes and feelings to which it is attached continue reflexively to trigger corrective reactions, which overtake that resolution.

Thus for the father in the case just described—still obsessively dutiful, after all—the very awareness of the sensation of freedom and relief that has come with the particular articulation of his conflict will, as its nature and its further expressions extend in consciousness, turn that sensation of freedom into an anxious and repugnant sensation of selfishness. In short, no conflict is a discrete event; it always embodies the personality's general attitudes and dispositions. Hence, no therapeutic articulation or resolution of a particular conflict—no more one that seems deep than one that may seem superficial—can in itself be regarded as final or complete.

There is another fundamental way, in addition to the corrective reaction of restrictive attitudes, that the personality's resistance to change expresses itself in psychotherapy: the *assimilation* of the new awareness—or of the therapeutic process itself—to the existing attitudes. The process depends, like the corrective reaction, on the person's unavoidable experience of the new according to his old attitudes. The clearest instances of such assimilation are comparatively simple and direct. I have mentioned them before, and they are completely familiar to every therapist.

A compulsive patient is at first quite struck by the realization that she is only able to make a personal decision comfortably when she can refer to authoritative rules of some sort, and that she does not seem to respect—often not even to consider—what she may like to do. Shortly afterward, however, it is apparent that she has transformed this realization into a new rule, without being aware of doing so. She now searches herself for clues to what she "really wants" to do, with the feeling that she must satisfy the rules of mental health.

Another such patient says, after a short silence during which he looks rather agonized, "I'm trying to figure out what I *want* to talk about. Because I know I should talk about what I want to talk about here. Isn't that right?"

Another patient, an intimidated and impressionable young woman, seems quite interested in the idea, suggested by the therapist, that she is often buffaloed by the authority of her impressive husband. She even seems to begin to talk about him more objectively. At the next session, however, she says eagerly, "Well, I spoke up last night, just like you told me to." The new, supposedly liberating idea has been transformed into a directive by another male authority.

As this case illustrates, the assimilation of therapeutic experience by existing attitudes is not limited to the therapeutic content but includes the therapeutic relationship. In this sense, transference may be regarded as such an assimilation.

(It is worth noting that the assimilation of initially inimical and disturbing experience to existing attitudes is not limited to psychotherapy. A striking example is the change I mentioned earlier in the delusional experience of the paranoid but still rigidly dutiful Schreber. At first horrified by the "voluptuous" female sensations in his body, he later accepted this transformation with equanamity when he understood it was his duty to God. The process of rationalization is certainly involved here, but that process is much too narrowly conceived as an intellectual one to encompass the general phenomenon of assimilation that is involved.)

Sometimes one can see not only the results of a process of assimilation, but also the process itself during the therapy hour. A case to which I referred earlier (see chapter 4) is an example. A new idea and interest are assimilated by the old attitude and its interests:

The young woman, an architect, is visibly depressed despite her initial briskness. She presents her problem as one of being too "challenging" and "harsh," not "feminine," "receptive," and "soft" enough. She is particularly concerned that she "can't hold on to a boyfriend," but she also makes it plain that she herself is "turned off" by these traits of hers. However, when the therapist suggests that her idea of what she should be like ("feminine") seems rather conventional, even old-fashioned, she seems surprised and interested.

After a time the therapist remarks that there is another way than hers to look at her problem. While she seems to feel that she is unsatisfactory because she is "challenging" and "harsh," he suggests, perhaps the problem can be understood the other way around. Perhaps she becomes "challenging" and

The Course of Therapeutic Change

"harsh"—touchy, actually—because she fears, to begin with, that she may be unsatisfactory.

She is clearly interested in this idea, perhaps even excited, and adds, "You mean, it's defensive, a sort of bravado." At this point, she relaxes noticeably. It seems that her new awareness of her attitude toward herself has diminished the force of that attitude. But a moment later she leans forward, once again full of urgent concern, and asks, "Then if therapy is successful, and I feel more secure, the harshness will be eliminated?" Her logic is sound, but the new idea has at least to some extent been put into the service of the old concern.

Some degree of assimilation of each new self-awareness to existing attitudes, like some degree of corrective reaction, is probably inevitable. Both would seem to follow, once again, from the fact that attitudes, not merely particular reactions, are being engaged by the therapeutic process. It is even quite possible that some such assimilation of the therapeutic experience may characterize an entire therapy, resulting in little or no change in attitudes at all. But, in general, the fact of such assimilation, like the larger fact of the personality's resistance to change, does not mean that a therapeutic effect has been totally canceled. This woman, for example, has had a new and relieving experience of herself. She has become conscious of herself in a different way, not merely as she is afraid she *appears*—as "harsh" and "turning people off"—but as she *feels*; and it is reasonable to suppose that she will not completely forget it. The evidence of assimilation of that experience to her existing attitudes at the same time only illustrates that therapeutic change is likely to proceed through a complex series of concessions and compromises.

The Concept of Resistance

I have used the term "resistance" so far in an impersonal and objective way, to describe the conservatism of the personality in the face of an external—that is, therapeutic—attempt to change it.[1] Resistance in this sense has no motive. It refers to a reactive tendency of the personality, not to an intentional action on the part of the person. In that sense the concept is an impersonal one. The personality's resistance to therapeutic change, including its capacity to assimilate inimical experience, is merely a special case of its self-regulating and self-stabilizing capacity.

It is true that the personality's resistance to change may *include* the generation of personal motives and intentional and quasi-intentional actions by the person as well. A resistance to disturbing change must certainly be a capacity and reactive tendency of all living organisms, but in the human organism, endowed with reflective consciousness, that capacity is extended to the formation of motives and acts. But these motives are not on the whole motives to resist change as such. They are motives and corrective actions aimed at dispelling the specific discomfort introduced by the particular change or threat of change. For instance, the discomforting sense of personal "selfishness" prompts a corrective action of renewed "considerateness" aimed at dispelling that discomfort. In the sense of resistance to change, therefore, the term "resistance" should probably be reserved to describe the general tendency of the

[1]For a like-minded view of resistance as a reflection of the neurotic personality as a "conservative organization," see Herbert J. Schlesinger, "Resistance as Process," in *Resistance: Psychodynamic and Behavioral Approaches*, ed. Paul Wachtel (New York: Plenum Press, 1981), pp. 24–44.

personality. The personal motivations or actions often generated by that tendency are of a more immediate sort and not so far-seeing.

From the standpoint of a therapeutic interest, particularly an impatient therapeutic interest, the neurotic personality's conservative tendencies and self-regulating capacities constitute a hindrance. But a more objective consideration of general adaptive requirements would suggest that the stability of the personality, even the neurotic personality, and its resistance to abrupt change, particularly in the adult, is adaptively essential. A human so constructed as to be easy to change would be altogether too plastic and impressionable. Such a human could never resist adversity.

All this is worth noting because the concept of resistance is an ambiguous one, endowed by its history with more than one meaning. To a large extent it has retained the meaning, once theoretically justifiable, of an obstacle to the therapeutic work erected by the patient. Thus it is still commonly used with the meaning of a "refusal" on the part of the patient to produce, or to permit access to, the therapeutic material, or even of a refusal to respond to the therapy in a satisfactory way.[2] This view, of course, can easily lead to an adversarial relationship with the patient, and to annoyance with him, in effect for continuing to be neurotic despite the therapist's efforts. At the same time, the theoretical developments of psychoanalysis— the recognition of the significance of the ego, specifically of the agencies of repression and defense—long ago justified a conception of resistance as itself constituting the largest part of the therapeutic material and of its analysis as the most decisive element of the therapeutic process. This conception of resist-

[2]See Otto Fenichel, *The Psychoanalytic Theory of Neurosis* (New York: W. W. Norton, 1945), pp. 27–29.

ance was most explicit in Wilhelm Reich's work.[3] Standing somewhat equivocally between these two views is Freud's formulation that "the essential part" of the psychoanalytic process lies in "the overcoming" of resistances.[4]

It seems apparent that the meaning and connotation of resistance will vary according to the theoretical view of neurosis and, in particular, of what constitutes the therapeutic material. The conception of resistance as an obstacle to the therapeutic work has a clear meaning if the therapeutic material is thought to consist simply of the repressed infantile memories. That concept of resistance becomes ambiguous, yet still sustainable, when the definition of the therapeutic material is enlarged to include the agency of repression or defense itself, as long as the neurotic problem is identified with particular infantile conflicts preserved and separated from the rest of the personality. (In that case, as a manifestation of a specific defense, resistance is therapeutic material; as avoidance of the identified problem or of material derived from the nuclear conflict, it is an obstruction.) But when the neurotic condition is seen as characterological and the patient himself as the therapeutic material, the obstacle conception of resistance loses all meaning.

Anna Freud observed that the patient cannot follow the basic rule beyond a certain point; we can press her argument further. It is not only that the patient may refuse to talk about this or avoid that, knowingly or unknowingly, as all patients do. More important, he will regularly talk in ways that distort the quality of his subjective experience. He will talk at length about what he is not interested in, thinking that he is; say what he does not fully believe, with an excess of apparent conviction,

---

[3]Wilhelm Reich, *Character Analysis* (New York: Orgone Institute Press, 1949).
[4]Sigmund Freud, "Psychoanalysis" (encyclopedia article, 1922), *Standard Edition*, 18:249 (London: Hogarth Press, 1955).

searching the eyes of the therapist for confirmation; talk more enthusiastically, or gloomily, or stoically than he feels; say, and think, he is simply angry when he actually feels ashamed; or declare that the therapy, like the rest of his life, is a failure while he is confirming the next appointment. His communication will be distorted in such ways because he deceives himself in such ways. All of this would be a serious impediment to the therapy if we relied on him to provide us, in what he said, with a window to his mind. But it is no impediment at all when it is recognized as the therapeutic material itself, as expressions of the workings of the neurotic personality.

From this standpoint, resistance still retains its impersonal meaning referring to the conservatism of the personality, the personality's general resistance to change; and in this sense the term can reasonably refer to the corrective reactions and assimilative processes I have described. It is also presumably true that one individual's personality will be comparatively more resistant to therapeutic effort than another's; but that is not an effect of, and cannot be reliably measured by, the individual's attitude toward the therapeutic process or therapeutic change as he sees it. As between the patient who is initially too ashamed to talk about his sex habits; and another patient who never misses an hour but declares at the beginning of each that he does not intend to be turned into "a happy idiot"; and yet another who is reassured by the role of patient, as he sees it, and dutifully plugs away at presenting "material," there is no basis to predict whose therapy will be longer or whose more successful. None of these reactions is in any case an impediment to the therapy, unless in the empty sense of calling the existence of an illness an impediment to its cure; each expresses the limitations and distortions of communication and relationships that are the therapy's subject matter; and in no sense is therapeutic attention to those distortions and limitations merely preliminary to that subject matter.

Sometimes a student describes an encounter with a patient that is quite successful, in which he has introduced the patient to himself and in the process made contact with him. The patient, who earlier had not known what he felt and clearly did not wish to know, was now able and even eager to talk, to say what was on his mind. After describing this event, the student asks what he should do then. What—when the patient finally discovers what he thinks or feels and wants to talk about what he had previously wanted to avoid—should the student "do with it"? The question contains a misunderstanding. When, on such an occasion, the patient even momentarily meets himself and discovers what he feels and wants to do, or what he has felt and needed to do, when he can talk about it and wants to talk about it, the therapeutic work is for that moment done. The communicative contact and the continued articulation of the patient's feelings that are achieved then are its products.

The Course of Therapy

Therapy is a work of particulars, not generalities. It follows the patient's interests and concerns in the particulars of his life. It is, therefore, by no means an unfavorable reflection on the therapist if he is unable to describe in any systematic and overall way the course of a therapy, even a successful one. Why should he be able to? He will have responded session by session to the patient as he seems at the time. His work does not require a preconceived plan, only an interest in what confronts him each session. (Such therapeutic plans are, it is true, sometimes worked out at staff conferences, but rarely, I imagine, is a serious attempt made to follow them.) Sometimes it is objected that this way of proceeding—following the patient wherever his concerns and his interests lead, and in that sense allowing him to set the direction of the therapy—is too circuitous a route to the neurotic problem. It is sometimes held to be too leisurely for the frequently limited time available for psychotherapy. Such objections have usually been answered, to my mind correctly, with the observation that there is no more direct route to the neurotic problem than what is on the patient's mind. Any attempt to penetrate "directly" to what the therapist may assume to be the problem, even as modest an effort of that sort as returning the patient to the serious concerns of the last session, will only waste time, not save it. This does not mean, of course, that the patient is left to find his way alone to the actual nature of his neurotic problem or of his unrecognized concerns. It is intrinsic to their nature that he needs the therapist's help for that.

The fact that the therapy proceeds according to the patient's interests and concerns, and not the therapist's design, is not inconsistent with its taking a describable and meaningful course according to the logic of its own development. It does seem to follow, though, that anything we may learn about that "natural" course of the therapy, the course that it takes of its own accord, will have no prescriptive or practical use for the therapist. It would not seem to help him to make plans, but only to confirm that it is unnecessary for him to do so. At least, that seems to be logical enough; but actually the matter is not so conclusive, and it involves some important and familiar clinical problems.

It might easily be argued that if there is a "natural" course of therapeutic progress, one that is determined essentially by the structure of the neurotic condition, then it had better be understood and followed systematically. It might be argued that for the therapist to fail to facilitate the therapeutic development along that course, or inadvertently to interfere with it, is to invite or actually create a miscarriage of the therapeutic process. In fact, Wilhelm Reich introduced his emphatically systematic "resistance analysis" with exactly this argument.[5] The therapeutic problem is by no means only of historical interest. It is a general problem even today for therapists and students of therapy.

Freud's recommendation had been to follow the lead of the patient. The effect of Reich's argument was to make clear that Freud's recommendation was not as simple and unambiguous as it might seem. For, he pointed out, the patient might very well provide "a wealth of material" deriving from different "levels," suggesting different themes. It was entirely possible that the patient's associations might contain material for a variety of interpretations that the patient was in no way prepared to understand or accept. It was, in short, all too easy for the analyst to get lost in the "wealth of material," to give interpretations of derivatives of the infantile neurosis when they would be completely ineffective, and in doing so, Reich thought, even to destroy their value for the future. This state of affairs was what Reich described as a "confused" or "chaotic" therapeutic situation. The only way to avoid it, he maintained, was to give priority always and systematically to the analysis of the resistance, by which he meant the characterological resistance. In that way, the analysis would proceed according to the "stratification" of the neurosis, reversing, he assumed, its genetic development.

[5]Reich, *Character Analysis* [3].

The Course of Therapeutic Change

The consensus among analysts at the time and subsequently has been that Reich went too far in his expectation of an orderly and "stratified" therapy. It has been generally recognized that he greatly underestimated the complexity of human psychology, not to speak of the effects on the patient of unpredictable circumstances of life. But if his conception of an orderly and "stratified" therapy was unrealistic, his recognition of the "confused" or "chaotic" therapeutic situation was not. It was, however, laid out in terms that make its general significance difficult to recognize.

The "chaotic" therapeutic situation that Reich identified as a problem of content interpretation, or interpretation of "meaning," made out of order, or before the resistance had been cleared away, actually reflects a more general therapeutic problem, one with which we are already familiar. It is a matter not merely of an incorrect sequence of interpretation, but of interpretation of *what* is said—of the content of associations or the narrative or the problem that is presented—without reference to its present relation to the speaker, without reference to how it is said, the purpose for which it is said, or the degree and kind of interest with which it is said. It is a result of the therapist's having followed the patient's words, perhaps all too eagerly, but having lost track of the patient. And it consists of the therapist's leading both the patient and himself into a consideration of subject matter that is, at best, simply not of interest, or not of the kind of interest at the moment that both patient and therapist suppose it to be.

Such situations are without doubt very common in therapy, though they are usually not as dramatic as Reich's description of them as "chaotic" would suggest. They are more often simply tedious. In fact, it is likely that to some degree such situations arise, perhaps repeatedly, in the course of every therapy. On the other hand, Reich's picture of a proper therapy as perfectly sequenced and orderly led him to overestimate the destructiveness of such problems. Contrary to Reich's warnings, there is no apparent reason why such a situation cannot be corrected. The therapist need only return his interest to the patient sitting before him.

The Nature of Therapeutic Progress

If not through Reich's orderly and "stratified" stages, what is the nature of therapeutic progress? If we claim to diminish the patient's estrangement from himself, to diminish the consciousness-distorting reactions of the personality to itself, is this achieved in an approximately continuous way, or through certain stages of enlargement of self-awareness?

It is possible to discern such stages in the changing attitude of a patient to whom I have referred before (see chapter 6), a well-educated, elderly woman, toward her drinking. I do not wish to describe the therapist's work here, but only to indicate the several stages of progress in this patient's increasing contact with herself.

When the patient entered treatment shortly after her husband's death, she wished it to be understood clearly that she did not regard herself as a patient in the ordinary sense. She stated that she merely wanted, now that her husband was dead, to have a person outside her intimate circle to whom she "could talk" as the occasion arose. Her own circle, she explained, mostly much younger than she, depended on her for support; she did not feel she should turn to them. On the contrary, she emphasized her "responsibility" to them. The therapist did not question her motivation. The patient did not speak of her drinking.

She at first vaguely explained her occasional absences, always without notice or message, as being due to illness. But it was in connection with an absence that she finally spoke of her drinking for the first time. She did not speak of it as a problem in any intrinsic sense but, rather haughtily, as a kind of accident. She did not know, she said, what happened on those occasions. She merely took a glass or two of sherry and then, some time later, realized that she had apparently drunk "too much" or "more than she wanted." In other words, she acknowledged the fact but completely denied the intention. It was apparent that she denied the intention not only to the therapist but also to herself.

She thus affected, at this point, a manner of rather lofty unconcern about the drinking problem, but only with an effort. In the course of the therapy, her awareness of this effort gradually increased and that artificial manner was sporadically, but increasingly, abandoned. For the first time, in fact, she expressed a profound disgust with herself. Nevertheless, at this time she spoke of her drinking only as a kind of moral failure, a reflection of a lack of willpower or even a lack of "common sense." She thought of it as a failing or a lapse—as the absence of something, in other words—but never quite as the presence of a wish or an intention to get drunk. She acknowledged such a failing, but distinguished it from *her*. Thus, her disgust was not precisely disgust with herself, but disgust and contempt for what she considered an "infantile" part of herself.

She said emphatically, "Something *in* me, something *infantile* wants to [drink], but *I* don't want to!"

Among the reasons she presented as to why *she* did not and would not want to drink, she mentioned one in particular: that it "failed her responsibility" to her circle of friends and caused them great concern. Thus she felt contempt for this "infantile part" of her that did not seem to recognize that responsibility, and she felt that contempt from the standpoint of the devoted and "responsible" friend that she regarded herself as being.

In the next stage there were two striking changes, largely as a result of the therapist's articulation of her moralistic contempt for human weakness. First, she spoke more openly, though still with disapproval, of her drinking. At the same time, she spoke quite differently of her circle of friends. One day, in an abrupt and emotional abandonment of her lofty and disapproving attitude toward her own drinking and her supposed neglect of her responsibility to her friends, she said with feeling that actually she is alone, that the people she had described as friends were only her husband's friends and "don't give a damn" about her, nor does she about them.

In the last stage I wish to describe, the patient talked less moralistically about her drinking and her wish to anesthetize herself and, consequently, more realistically about the present circumstances that prompt it. At the same time she moderated her judgments about her friends, distinguishing among various individuals, for some of whom what she said was true and others with whom there was actual friendship.

I have tried to distinguish several stages of the patient's increased awareness of her own feelings and purposes, increasingly objective recognition of her circumstances, and, also, increasing communicative contact with the therapist. I do not mean to suggest that such stages are absolutely discrete or orderly. They overlap greatly, are constantly reversed, and, as in this case, may actually sometimes be compressed, temporarily, in an hour or two. Still, in a general way, they describe a sequence with a direction. These stages could not have been predicted and, I think, could not have been circumvented. The reason they could not have been circumvented is simple. The therapist can only talk to the patient as she is at the present moment: at first about her effortful denials; then, when it becomes evident, about the moralistic contempt for herself that triggers those denials, and so forth. Even if he could have foreseen what was to come, he could not have accelerated the process.

The following case illustrates stages of progress that are in some ways comparable. The patient is a forty-two-year-old divorced woman, a musician, who has an adolescent daughter. She has been depressed following a medically required removal of both fallopian tubes (salpingectomy). In this case also it is possible to discern several stages in the patient's increased awareness of her own feelings and an increased clarity of expression, as initially unrecognized feelings of shame and inadequacy are articulated.

Initially, the patient sees her problem and presents it as an uncomplicated reaction to an objective shock. It is now "final," she says, as it has not been before, that she will "never have any more children." There is no question about the reality of her depression—she sounds and looks very depressed—yet the way in which she says that she knows now she will "never have any more children" sounds somewhat artificial, as if rehearsed.

What is actually on her mind soon becomes clear from what she actually talks about. It is not life without more children (which, in fact, is the life she has preferred for many years) but an altered image of herself. It turns out, in other words, that the objective circumstance—no more children—that she has identified as the problem has a different significance, a significance for her image of herself, which she has not recognized. She arrives at a different articulation of her feelings. She now speaks of having become a "barren" woman and says that she cannot any longer fulfill "the basic function of a woman." It is clear that this formulation is a closer representation of her feelings, containing in particular some expression of her feelings of shame and insufficiency. Yet this formulation too sometimes sounds exaggerated and artificial, like a quotation, not her own style of speech.

Soon thereafter she arrives at a new formulation of her feelings, one that sounds more genuine. She says, "What man would want a woman who couldn't even have children?" In this formulation, the further significance of "barrenness" for her is more clearly expressed. It also expresses the subjective form of her feelings of insufficiency and sense of shame in the concern about what *men* will think. On that point, she often tries to reassure herself by counting her "pluses": her education, her accomplishments, her good looks. She counts them as if she were counting her dowry.

The mention by the therapist on various occasions of such efforts to reassure herself elicits still another formulation of the feelings and concern triggered by her surgery. Since the operation, she now says, she feels—and fears she looks—old. A puzzling feature of the original clinical picture now becomes clear. She had seemed to be in fairly good spirits for some three or four weeks after the operation, only then, rather abruptly, becoming depressed. Now she recalls that it was then that she noticed that she had put on weight and, she adds uncertainly, that "age spots" had appeared on the back of her hands.

Thus, in each of her formulations, in each revision, the patient comes closer to articulating the actual quality of her depressive feelings. Each formulation seems to give these feelings a less external, less oblique expression and at the same time seems more direct in its communication. In the course of time, still other components of these feelings emerge, some long antedating her surgery. For example, she had been concerned with her weight off and on since adolescence, and on that account, among various others, had long felt unattractive.

Very often, as neurotic attitudes and their subjective dynamics are articulated and gradually relaxed—I am thinking particularly of obsessively conscientious attitudes—symptomatic improvement takes an interesting course. The symptom in these cases, such as an obsessive symptom, does not merely diminish gradually in intensity or gradually become less preoccupying while remaining otherwise the same. Not only does the content of the symptom change as it diminishes in intensity but to a certain extent the form does as well. The symptom changes from one whose reasons are more estranged and subjectively mysterious to one that is subjectively familiar and acceptable. To put it another way, the change is from an extreme, perhaps even bizarre, symptom to a behavior or reaction that embodies the same attitudes but may be so familiar as hardly to be recognized as a symptom at all.

For example, a young man's obsessional concerns originally required him to perform various extraordinary rituals, the purpose of which was quite lost to him, such as the daily wearing of special pins in various places on his clothing (somewhat in the spirit of tying a string on the finger as a reminder) and the carrying of various amulets. Later, these rituals disappeared; he gradually lost interest in them. Yet he continued to *worry* abundantly about decisions, job insecurities, and the like. But his obsessive worries seemed reasonable to him on the whole, in marked contrast to his view of the original obsessive symptoms.

In such a case, it appears that the original ritualistic symptoms, though products of familiar attitudes, are subjectively unrecognizable because they are end-products of the complicated workings of these relentlessly conscientious attitudes. Precautionary measures are compounded by further precautionary measures, becoming more and more distant from recognizable concerns. As the dynamics of these attitudes are articulated and they are gradually relaxed, the "microgenesis" of the symptom does not extend as far as it originally did. Hence, the more complicated and remote products of that microgenesis disappear first, while the attitudes and precautionary purposes themselves emerge in more recognizable forms and the anxieties that trigger them unfold.

Another obsessive patient, a twenty-five-year-old businessman, in a symptomatic reaction that is not rare, has become quite agitated with concern that he might "slip over the edge" and become schizophrenic or, even worse, that he already has. This concern is the product of a cycle of obsessive concerns, the anticipation of various possible calamities having led to notice of his own anxious thinking and the anticipation, then, of a calamity of the thinking itself.

The gradual articulation and relaxation of this obsessive worry leads to its reformulation. He now says that he fears he might become schizophrenic if he were to allow himself to relax his anxious concentration and self-control; in other words, if he were not to assume the worst, the danger would be greater. Later—less distressed, his precautionary anticipations less extreme—his concern is that if he were to relax his worry, he might not get enough work done, might allow his business to dwindle. Still later, he expresses the anxiety that if he abandons his worry he might even slip into complacency and, in that way, his life might "go right down the pleasure drain."

As restrictive, consciousness-distorting attitudes are articulated and relaxed and the patient's awareness of his actual feelings is increased, existing relationships are likely to come into sharper focus. In this way, changes in external relationships can mark stages of internal change. Sometimes there is a succession of such changes within the same relationship. The awareness of previously unrecognized feelings and a new, clearer perception of an existing relationship will then be followed by the further articulation of those feelings, the discovery of further components of them and further dynamics within them. For the therapist at least, the process is somewhat like looking through a microscope whose magnification is increased in stages. What had been a dark, blurred spot in the object turns out on magnification to have a structure; it is complicated and contains some sharply defined areas of various colors. The focus then shifts to one of these colored areas that had previously been an invisible component of a larger area and, with a further increase of magnification, that area also turns out to be differentiated. Furthermore, it may happen that the structure of this newly visible area bears some formal similarity to the structure of the previous, less magnified image. It has been organized according to the same or related principles.

For example, a middle-aged man, married and with one child, enters therapy in considerable distress over a tangled personal life. For the past few months, he says, he has had an exciting sexual and romantic relationship with a young woman whom he loves. He has resolved to stop seeing her many times, he says, but he "cannot" stop. He "knows" that he "must give this up," however, because he will not, "could not," leave his wife and child, whom he also loves ("in a different way") and could not hurt. He has come to therapy, he says, to "learn [how] to give up" his affair and, perhaps, to feel once again a romantic and sexual interest in his wife. He speaks of these aims, however—particularly the latter one—with a noticeable absence of hope and, perhaps, of genuine interest. In short, it seems, the patient comes to be reformed, to be somehow gotten to do what he thinks he should do but does not want and probably does not intend to do. I shall describe only a single phase of the therapy.

Soon after the therapy begins, the patient discovers, to his surprise, that the therapist has no special interest in reforming him. No doubt this fact contributes to his increased awareness of the half-heartedness of his own interest in reform. He becomes aware of the oppressively dutiful (and therefore resentful) components of his feelings about his wife. He soon feels freer and less repentant about his continuing romantic relationship, and he begins seriously and frankly to consider leaving his wife in order to marry his lover.

At this point, however, his feelings take an unexpected turn (though not in retrospect a remarkable one). It becomes noticeable that his enthusiasm for his lover and their romantic relationship has diminished, though at first he is reluctant to admit it. Gradually, he expresses certain reservations about her: she calls too often, sometimes to the point of being a nuisance; she is perhaps too dependent on him. It becomes evident that as his dutiful attitude toward his wife has been articulated and has relaxed, the romantic aura of his affair has begun to fade. The romantic and sexual excitement of that relationship had apparently been an aspect of its vaguely sinful nature and its unavailability and faded as the relationship came into sharper and more objective focus.

It becomes obvious that he is increasingly tempted to end relations with his lover completely, yet he does not immediately do so. The first reason he gives for his reluctance is that he does not want to hurt her. The second and, it seems, more important reason is familiar in its general attitude but new in its content. To end the affair, he says, would be to "surrender to the rocking chair," a "copout." He has, he says, a "duty" to himself to consider. He means that he has a responsibility to "live life to the fullest" (whether he wants to or not), not to "waste" life. It is clear that this dutiful attitude, not yet articulated, had also been responsible for his reluctance even to recognize his growing disaffection from her.

Thus there is a striking reversal of attitude toward the two women. It occurs in two stages. The one who was originally the forbidden, vague, and romantic figure first comes into focus as a person and then quickly becomes an object of duty and responsibility. The one who originally represented family responsibility now comes to represent, not romance to be sure, but another kind of improper temptation, a kind of domestic comfort that is "copping out."

The reversal of roles, though striking, is not itself of great significance. It marks the stages of change with unusual clarity, but it is essentially an accident of the particular circumstances. Originally not just one but both women are, in effect, vague representations of different responsibilities: family responsibility on the one hand, and responsibility to "live life to the fullest" on the other. Neither is clearly articulated, but he is pressed by both. But it is initially the domestic responsibility, the one more present, that is the more burdensome, casting his lover as its romantic antithesis. The articulation and relaxation of the most immediate focus of his sense of responsibility, that to his wife, brings both women—brings the situation—into sharper and more objective focus. It also permits a closer view of his feelings about his affair. These feelings turn out to include attitudes much like those of his relationship with his wife. In other words, here too he has been driven by a sense of responsibility to a rule of living. Nevertheless, he is now somewhat less driven and somewhat closer to a condition of knowing his mind.

This last case also illustrates that such stages as the therapy encounters cannot be chosen or circumvented by the therapist but are determined by the personality, and situation, of the patient. The therapist can only contribute to the articulation of that conflict or its components as it is expressed at a particular time.

The following case, which I introduced in chapter 2, illustrates that point in a somewhat more extended way. It shows, as well, the unfolding, through several stages, of the subjective dynamics of the neurotic conflict. By this I mean that it is possible to discern several stages of the patient's anxious and reflexive reaction against his own feelings, as he becomes aware of them. These stages appear to reflect the successive phases of self-estrangement that have progressively removed him from awareness of his feelings and have finally resulted in a symptomatic reaction which he cannot understand. The unfolding of these dynamics is a far cry from the sort of stratification that Reich had in mind. It will tell us nothing—at least directly— about the etiology of the neurotic personality. But it has much to say about its present workings and the construction of its symptomatic forms.

The patient resembles the patient I have just considered, both in his general obsessive character and in the nature of the principal symptom; but the symptom in this case is more severe. The attitudes and aims that give subjective sense and reason to the patient's obsessive idea are further removed from his awareness; his behavior is therefore more ritualistic; and the experience is probably considerably more painful. This brief presentation will consider only the development of the patient's self-awareness in connection with the specific symptom for which he has sought help, an intense and originally agonizing obsessive regret.

As I described earlier, the patient, an attorney in his late forties, is obsessed by the thought, which he initially calls "crazy," that he has irreparably ruined his life by his failure to pursue and marry a certain woman he had known briefly many years before. Although he initially speaks of his obsession as a "crazy" or an "insane" preoccupation that he cannot "shake," it is apparent that he is actually by no means sure that the idea is so crazy. Even when he speaks with exasperation of the absurdity of such an infatuation with "someone [he] hardly knew!" he never looks quite convinced of its absurdity. Indeed he speaks, as though speaking to himself, with just that kind of urgent emphasis ("It's ridiculous!") one might use in trying to convince someone, trying to get that fact across to someone, who stubbornly refuses to believe it. The therapist, as the occasion arises, says as much.

On one such occasion, the patient seems to get the point. He seems to recognize that in fact he does not really believe what he says so emphatically, and he relaxes somewhat—but only momentarily. He straightens up and continues: But he *should* cut this out and be sensible! He *should* see that it is all nonsense! After all he hardly knew her! He should forget it and be happy with what he has! This, he adds, is what every one of those people who know his story has told him, and he agrees with them! They all say it's nonsense!

But, the therapist suggests, all of that—the fact that *they* say it's nonsense; his feeling that he *should* agree that it's nonsense—is not the same thing as actually believing that it *is* nonsense.

At that point the patient becomes silent, as if at last despairing of further efforts to persuade himself that it is "nonsense" and that he "should forget" it. Perhaps he also despairs of ridding himself of the obsession in that way—more or less by force—which is the only way he can imagine being rid of it.

It soon becomes clear that in his private and hardly articulated view—as opposed to the view he dutifully tries to persuade himself of—the idea is far from nonsense. For the first time now he speaks of the woman herself: she was beautiful and vivacious.

It becomes noticeable, on the occasion of such a description, that he has surprisingly little to say about her and that what he does say is, for the most part, quite vague and abstract. The listener can have no idea, apart from a few details, what she is like. The therapist remarks on this, and eventually suggests that she seems to be more an idea to him than a person. The observation is brushed off.

He resumes, as he often does, with an emphatic gloominess. Almost with a groan, he asks, How *could* he have let this chance slip through his fingers?

The therapist remarks that that certainly does not sound like a question but a reproach. Still, the therapist continues, since he has asked, if he didn't pursue her, he must have had his reasons at the time.

For a moment the patient's expression changes. It is as if a new idea has been presented, obvious as it is. What is striking to him, surely, is the attitude to his "mistake" embodied in this simple idea, a psychological attitude of understanding rather than the moral reproach he is accustomed to. He becomes more relaxed and seems interested in this point of view. Watching him, one almost expects him to declare that he had not pursued her because he simply had not found her that appealing.

But nothing of the sort happens. He straightens up and resumes his reproaches against himself: He doesn't *know* why he didn't try! It was probably his damned neurotic hesitation and fear! He has missed his chance!

He continues to underscore the point, the cost of his mistake, by recounting the numerous occasions during the day on which he is reminded of her. The therapist observes that he seems not only to be reminded of her on these occasions but, once reminded, to find it necessary to pull out the complete file on his mistake and its consequences, to rub it in, to punish.

Again he is briefly interested, but he quickly continues: "I must stop this! . . . But I can't!" He hints, as he has before, that the only relief might be suicide; but at this point his agony seems somewhat forced, certainly not deliberately false, but somewhat worked up and lacking conviction. There is no doubt, however, that he tortures himself not only with the idea that his life will be ruined by his mistake but also that it will be ruined by the obsession itself. He continues: He has had his chance and blown it! *How,* he wants to know, *how* can he forget that?

The therapist remarks that when he says, *"How* can I forget it?" in that way, as he often does, he seems to mean not so much that it is impossible to forget it as that it would be wrong, impermissible, to forget it.

The patient's response to this observation is striking. He indignantly charges the therapist with advocating, at least by implication, an attitude of irresponsibility. He demands to know how anyone could, after a terrible mistake, simply shrug his shoulders and "walk away from it"! On various subsequent occasions he scornfully characterizes such an attitude as one of passive resignation (a willingness to be satisfied with anything that comes along, in contrast to an active pursuit of opportunities); smug complacency (a kind of cocky self-satisfaction in contrast to an attitude of scrupulous self-criticism); or heedless and indifferent willingness to take "the easy way out."

It becomes increasingly apparent, when he speaks of this woman's attractions, that his praises are rather forced; they do not carry conviction. His reaction to the therapist's remark to this effect is curious. He grudgingly acknowledges that "sometimes" this "might" be so, that he "might" sometimes exaggerate her attractiveness, but so what? It is a small matter and means nothing. Why make something out of it?

It gradually becomes clear that the patient's attitude distorts his judgment in this matter in ways that reflect his familiar scrupulousness. He is only concerned, in connection with this woman as in other things, that he might *undervalue* an opportunity, treat it too lightly or, as he puts it, too "complacently," taking "the easy way out." Even if he might—he makes it clear that he is not ready to say more than "might"—sometimes have doubts that she was actually so wonderful, he fears saying so or even allowing himself to think so. For he might then drift into complacency (that is, release himself from further repentance) when it is not certain that such a release is justified. It becomes clear that when he senses such doubts in himself about her, he becomes uneasy about the possibility of a "complacent" underestimation of his loss. At such times he immediately attempts to correct himself by reminders of her attractions. In his obsessive scrupulousness he practices in this way a kind of personal thought control, without being aware of it, and consistently distorts his own judgment. He consistently leans over backward, in his evaluation of missed opportunities, to avoid any possibility that he is dismissing regrets too easily or taking "the easy way out."

I have tried to show here the gradual articulation of a single aspect of this patient's subjective world. It was accompanied by the gradual diminishing of his obsessive symptom. (At the point that the symptom was essentially gone—after approximately two and a half years of weekly sessions—the patient chose to end the treatment.) Such progress is never orderly, but it is possible to identify certain stages in it.

The patient's initial view of his obsessive idea may be expressed as: I want to forget it, but I can't! ("I can't shake it"). At this point, the symptom is regarded only as an inexplicable, painful, and exasperating compulsion ("It's ridiculous!" "Crazy!").

It quickly becomes apparent, however, that this helpless and exasperated view actually contains the reproachful attitude: I *should* forget it (but I can't)! His often repeated "It's ridiculous!" is uttered with that attitude: I *should* believe "it's ridiculous!"

The therapeutic articulation of that reproachful and consciousness-distorting reaction is followed by a relaxation of it and a clearer awareness of his feelings, approximately as follows: Everyone tells me that it's ridiculous and that I should forget it, but I am not sure that I want to.

The relaxation of his reproachful attitude toward his preoccupation actually has two effects: first, he realizes that he does not want to forget; second, the object of that regret, the woman, for the first time begins to come into focus. Thus, there is some recovery of the emotional basis for his regret ("She was beautiful . . ."). At this point, the obsession becomes subjectively much less mysterious and alien. However conflicted and peculiar, it has begun to have a sense of personal reasonableness.

The restoration of the patient's awareness of his interest, not in forgetting but in remembering, and the emergence of the object of that interest bring to light in turn something of that interest's dynamics. Its forced quality becomes particularly apparent. Thus in the last stage I describe, the attitude the patient expresses is approximately: Even if I could forget the mistake, I *shouldn't.* And further: Even if I'm not sure that it *was* a mistake, I should assume it was. From the patient's exaggeratedly scrupulous point of view, it is not merely wrong and impermissible to forgive the neglect of such an opportunity; it is wrong and impermissible even to doubt its value. The gradual articulation of this attitude, which actually occupied most of the therapy, brought to awareness the motivation for his obsessive remorse and dissolved its alien and mysterious nature. Whereas he had initially said, in effect, I *should* forget about her (even though I think I loved her), it now becomes clear that he actually felt, I *should not* forget about her (if I might possibly have loved her). This awareness completes the transformation of the obsessive thought from an experience of irrational compulsion to one of intentional repentance prompted by his familiar scrupulousness. The regretful thought, in other words, can now be recognized by him as another duty that it would be heedless, irresponsible, and complacently self-satisfied to neglect.

This development represents a progressive diminishing of the patient's estrangement from his own subjective world; a diminishing of the distortion of his self-awareness; and an increasingly focused and objective view of the figure of his obsessive preoccupation. With respect to his obsessional symptom, this progression implies an increasing sense of its authorship and its intentionality, hence a diminishing of its driven or obsessive quality.

The particular stages in this progress follow an understandable program. They consist largely of the successive articulations of the patient's corrective and consciousness-distorting reactions to his own feelings. Each such reaction distorts his awareness of those feelings; each successful articulation of the dynamics involved brings him a step closer to awareness of his feelings. Thus, the initial articulation of his attitude: I *should* believe it's all ridiculous (when, in fact, he does not believe it is ridiculous); the further articulation of: How *can* I forget such a mistake? (as actually meaning that he *should not* allow himself to forget); and the later articulation of: I must not doubt that it was a mistake (reflecting, of course, the existence of such doubts)—each of these stages of articulation brings the patient closer to his actual feelings and judgment. At each level a similar distortion of self-awareness is articulated. In each case, that distortion consists of a rejection of what he feels or believes out of deference to what he thinks he should feel or believe—or, more precisely, out of an anxious sensation that he is not respectful or attentive enough to what he should feel or believe. In each case, the articulation of that distortion revives that anxiety and the articulation is accordingly resisted.

It may well be that the progress of therapy through these stages of diminished self-estrangement reverses the stages in which the obsessive symptom was constructed. If so, the presenting experience of the symptom as a "crazy" and compulsive idea is the product of successive reactions of the obsessively conscientious attitude to a series of anxious sensations of "complacency," "taking the easy way out," or disrespect for what the patient thinks he should feel or believe. Thus a neglected "opportunity" is glorified, after it is gone, in a spirit of self-reproach; the charge of negligence thereby constructed cannot be dismissed for fear of compounding the negligence; persistent concern for the possibility of such negligence can only be quieted by including ever more remote associative connections with the missed opportunity in the category of "reminders" that should not be ignored. In such a way, increasingly ritualistic obsessive regrets may be constructed, out of relentless scrupulousness, by the repeated reactions of the same scrupulous attitude to a series of subjective anxieties.

Of course, this describes only the development of a symptom in an already neurotic personality, not the development of the personality itself. Whether the development of a symptom is likely to offer some insight into the development of the neurotic character itself is an interesting question. Some facts suggest that it might. After all, if we observe that each particular stage in the therapeutic reversal of the symptom involves a relaxation of the general restrictive attitude, perhaps it can be supposed that the adult form of that attitude developed through comparable stages. Perhaps the ultimately relentless conscientious attitude, once its development is underway in childhood, works upon itself, makes any relaxation or reversal of its strictures abhorrent, and requires that they repeatedly extend themselves in order to dispel anxiety.

Terminating Therapy

I wish to consider two issues in connection with the ending of psychotherapy. The first is the question of when to end therapy and how that decision is made. To be sure, in a great many cases that issue does not arise at all. Nowadays the termination of therapy is very often determined by institutional policy, limitations of training periods, and other extrinsic factors. Nevertheless the issue does arise, typically in private practice, and it involves certain problems that are of more general interest. The second matter has to do with the patient's reaction to the end of therapy and the therapist's response to these reactions, however that decision has been made.

If one goes to a physician for treatment, there is as a rule no problem with who decides on a reasonable time to end the treatment or with the way the decision is made. In effect, the physician makes the decision, and he makes it on a technical basis. At least, the physician makes the recommendation, which—in almost all cases—a sensible person will follow. The reason for this is simple. The illness is an objective matter, and the judgment can only be made on the basis of objective facts—X-rays, blood count, and so forth—the significance of which is known to the doctor, not as a rule to the patient. The patient's subjective feeling may have some technical significance, but quite possibly none at all. The objective facts are decisive. In psychotherapy the situation is quite different, in some respects even reversed.

The fundamental aims of psychotherapy are not objective, but subjective. Whereas the physician is in most cases the logical authority on the success or failure, or on the degree of success, of his treatment and of its reasonable end point, in psychotherapy it is the patient who speaks with authority on such matters as whether he feels better, how much better, and how much distress remains. We cannot determine a reasonable completion of a patient's therapy, for example, on the basis of how much compulsiveness remains. We treat not diagnoses but the subjective distress that usually, but only quite approximately, is implied by them. Similarly, a reasonable point to end the therapy cannot be decided on the basis of whether a patient has left his wife or whether another patient is having a baby; the relevant facts are how the patients feel about what they are doing.

It is true that psychotherapy is often concerned with objective or quasi-objective symptoms—alcohol and drug dependency, phobias, problems of sexual function, work inhibition. But symptomatic improvement in that sense, while obviously important, is not a reliable guide to therapeutic achievement; and in a great many cases symptoms are of a sort that provides no objective guide at all. It is also true that various standards of mental health or maturity, often high-sounding, usually with mixed objective and subjective features, have been offered as guides for the termination of treatment. But such standards, as Edith Weigert put it, "can easily become impositions of the superego, which elicit self-deception and pretense."[6] The fact that such ambitions and standards of the therapist for his patients can easily become authoritative impositions implies, of course, that they are inimical to legitimate therapeutic goals. It also suggests that they are essentially presumptuous. Patients are not children and psychotherapy is not child rearing.

What, then, is the answer? Should the decision of when to end the therapy be regarded simply as the patient's responsibility, leaving in his hands, as the final authority, the issue of whether he feels good enough to stop or distressed enough to make it worthwhile to continue? At least as far as continuing treatment is concerned, this view was apparently the one that Sandor Ferenczi came to in his later years: "As long as the patient wants to come, he belongs in analysis."[7] Yet something seems wrong with this conclusion. However much the subjective nature of therapeutic aims may be argued, the fact remains that the therapist is in a position to have some judgment of their achievement. Quite apart from objective standards of supposed psychological health, he will have some impression

[6]Edith Weigert, "Contribution to the Problem of Terminating Psychoanalysis," *Psychoanalytical Quarterly* 21, no. 4 (1952): 479.
[7]Quoted in ibid., p. 465.

of the patient's frame of mind and the degree of his neurotic distress, not only from what the patient reports but from the general quality of his communication. Then, too, the therapist may have something to contribute to the decision on the basis not only of his knowledge of the patient but also of therapy. He may have something to say concerning what more might be expected, how long it might take, whether it makes sense to reduce the frequency of hours, whether the patient can return if he wishes, and such.

But there is a more fundamental question. How can we expect the neurotic patient to evaluate the state of his own feelings when, by definition, he very often does not know his own feelings and deceives himself about them? Self-deception is the very nature of the patient's neurotic problem. How, then, can such questions as "Do you feel better?" or "Do you feel good enough?" be referred to him for an answer? How can we expect of the one who deceives himself that he will know when he has stopped doing so?

The answer to this question points to the therapist's proper role in the matter. The fact that a patient's decision may be influenced by his neurotic problem is no reason to attempt to take that decision out of his hands. It certainly is reason, however, to continue the therapeutic work. For in the matter of this decision, as in general, the therapist has a more important (and less presumptuous) contribution to make than his judgment about the decision. He is in a position to see, as the patient is not, the patient's relation to that decision, his perspective on it—his self-deception, if it exists, in connection with it. The therapist is in a position to see how the patient talks about the question of termination: how he says what he says about it, or for that matter how he avoids it, if he seems to avoid it.

For example, a patient who obviously feels better seems at

times to cast about for "problems," yet not in the self-conscious way of many patients who feel obliged to produce "material." It turns out that he has thought of ending the therapy but, he says rather wistfully, he is "not ready yet." He explains: When he thinks of leaving, he "combs through" his mind for remaining problems. If he can find any, he feels he is not ready yet. It would be "hubris," he says, to declare himself satisfactory while he still has problems.

Another patient, somewhat better after a long period of therapy, increasingly presents himself as if for duty, grudgingly. Yes, he concedes, he may feel that way. Nonetheless, he "can't stop yet"; he still isn't happy. Doesn't that make sense, he asks, to continue until he is happy? The therapist responds that it might very well make sense, except that he does not look like a man who is here in the expectation, or even in the hope, of achieving happiness.

The therapeutic articulation of the patient's attitude toward the question of terminating treatment may lead to an agreement to bring the therapy to an end, or it may not. It will, however, make it possible to talk with the patient about his actual feelings and concerns. The therapist may indeed have questions to answer, opinions to offer, even judgments to make about matters such as the ones I have referred to in connection with termination. But it makes no sense merely to answer questions, offer opinions, or make judgments if they are in response to a premise—and therefore have a significance—that is unrecognized by both patient and therapist. Suppose, for example, the patient who feels it is impermissible to leave therapy as long as he has a blemish asks wistfully how much longer it may take to cure a certain symptom. It misses the point to discuss that question without recognizing that it is asked not out of longing for relief from the symptom's pain, but out of longing to satisfy therapeutic obligations.

The Course of Therapeutic Change

It will be evident that the principle implied here in connection with the decision about ending the therapy is the same one that has guided this book: the patient is the therapeutic material; pay attention not only to the problem the patient sees but also to the patient. That principle can also be applied to the second issue I mentioned, the patient's reaction to the termination of therapy once it has already been set.

In a sense, more attention is paid to the subject of the patient's reaction to termination than that subject requires. Preconceptions are engendered, in students at least, about the way the patient will react to the experience; and such preconceptions, even if they do not lead to insistent interpretations, can easily be an encumbrance. But there is a more specific problem that has to do with the particular nature of those preconceptions. It derives from the assumption, of a kind already familiar, that the patient's reaction to the termination of therapy is a revival and repetition of early experiences or fantasies, particularly of separation and loss. The assumption is that the adult reaction to termination consists of a direct triggering of unconsciously preserved childhood reactions or fantasies by the comparable therapeutic situation. Such an understanding, once again, circumvents the existence and the activity of an intervening adult personality. From our standpoint, on the contrary, an exaggerated or distorted reaction by the patient to the termination of therapy is a product of a neurotic personality, not the direct product of a preserved memory or fantasy. The distinction makes a practical difference.

The assumption that the present reaction is an effect and a repetition of an earlier one is consistent with, and may easily lead to, too narrow a view of the therapeutic material. That historical assumption is of an essentially passive revival of an earlier memory or fantasy represented in the patient's present picture of the termination. Accordingly, that picture (constructed from the patient's references and allusions to the event) becomes the therapeutic material. But a proper view of the therapeutic material does not consist merely of the patient's picture of an event; it consists, rather, of the present activity of the patient—the engagement of the dynamics of his personality by the event, the distortion of his awareness of his feelings about the event by those dynamics. Those ways in which—according to the dynamics of his personality—the patient may attempt, for example, to dispel anxiety in connection with the event, or to assimilate the event, will appear, as usual, not only in what the patient says about the event but in how he says it.

Thus, the obsessive patient continues to "comb through his mind" as the termination approaches, looking for remaining problems, testing his discomfort in the way one presses a tooth that has been sensitive but is now supposedly quiet. He presents the "problems" he finds with exaggerated concern. He is relieved to be at the end of therapy, but he does not know it. He does not dare to celebrate or to abandon his worry.

Another patient, when informed by his student-therapist of her coming departure, walks out, apparently angry. But his anger actually appears somewhat worked-up and unconvincing. He has seized on her announcement as if to underscore that she, too, has failed him.

That worry, now almost perfunctory, in the one case, and that defensive, worked-up anger and eagerness to prove a point, in the other, both express the dynamics of the personality and its attitudes as the event has engaged them. Each reaction, in its way, is a distortion of self-awareness. When the therapist and the patient articulate the subjective dynamics of such reactions, they will be talking about attitudes and feelings that are far more characteristic of the individual than general to the event of termination.

In short, the therapist's responsibility in connection with the patient's reaction to the termination of therapy is to continue to do what he has been doing all along. Even at the end of therapy, our aim is still to introduce the patient to himself. This persistence does not spring, as it may seem, from an unrelenting professionalism, nor even from the hope of contributing much further to the integration of the patient's personality. That would be worthwhile, of course, but it would be pointless to try to achieve at the very end much that has not been achieved already. We still want to introduce him to himself because, then at least as much as at any other time, we want to communicate with him. If there is a choice between a communicative contact with him on the one hand and an accommodation of his self-deception on the other, we choose the contact, even if that is momentarily discomforting to him. We do so, if for no other reason, because we do not like the alternative. We choose, if it comes to that, a genuine laugh between us at the patient's relief on reaching the end of his long sentence in preference to his artificial gratitude.

INDEX

Alliance, therapeutic, *see* Therapeutic alliance

Analytic situation, 101–2; patient's role in, 102, 103–5; *see also* Therapeutic relationship

Anxiety: articulation of particular, 196; development of restrictive attitudes and inhibitory reactions to, 38, 46–47; obsessive indecision and, 38–40; in reaction to self-awareness, 41–42; source of, 173–78; subjective experience of, 175–78

Aristotle, 117

Arms and the Man (Shaw), 154–56

Articulation of subjective experience, 139; of motivations, conscious, 33–34; of particular anxiety, 196; of patient's attitude toward terminating therapy, 230; polarity between the self and external world and, 123–32; of reaction to the self, 133–37; of tension, 119–23; therapeutic change through, 119–23; therapist's initiation of, 11–12, 132

Artificial self-confidence, 12–13

Assimilation of therapeutic experience by existing attitudes, 197–99

Associations: directed, 18, 54; free, 18, 54, 71, 165

Attitude(s): as embodied in actions, 41–42; assimilation of therapeutic

experience by existing, 197–99; change in, 193; distortion of self-awareness by, 32; of patient toward self, 102–5; of patient toward self, reaction to articulation of, 133–37; therapeutic, 151–57; *see also* Restrictive attitudes; Subjective experience

Austin, J. L., 62, 62*n*

Authority, patient's notion of therapist's, 101–2

Authorship, restoration of sense of, 121–23, 126

Basic rule of psychoanalysis, 53, 54, 55, 63, 158, 159, 160, 202

Berlin, Isaiah, 117

Biographical information, patient's presentation of, 79–80

Breuer, Josef, 15, 169

Censorship, second, 11*n*

Change, therapeutic, 13, 115–39, 192–233; articulation of subjective experience and, 119–23; course of therapy and, 204–8; development of self-awareness in childhood and, 137–39; nature of, 13; polarization and, 123–32;

Index

progress, nature of therapeutic, 208–26; reaction to self and, 133–37; resistance to, 193–99; resistance to, concept of, 200–204; self-understanding and, 117–19; terminating therapy and, 226–33; two distinct processes involved in, 193

"Chaotic" therapeutic situation, 206, 207–8

Character, neurotic, 14–50; dynamics of subjective experience and, xi, 36–50; loss of reality and, 33–36; symptomatic behavior, consciousness and self-estrangement in, 26–33

Character analysis, 56–57

Characteristic subjective world, 27

Characterological "ego deformity," 25–26

Characterological nature of neurosis, historical understanding vs., 168–73

Childhood: development of neurosis in, 177–78, development of self awareness in, 137–39; fantasied dangers of, 173–74; see also Historical interpretation

"Choice of neurosis," problem of, 20–21

Circularity in workings of neurotic personality, 131

Collaborative relationship, traditional, 159–64; change to communicative relationship from, 164–65; couch arrangement and ease of talking in, 163–64; patient's consciousness of role in, 160–63

Communication: contact with the self and with therapist, 141–51;

effective, 141; see also Speech acts; Therapeutic material

Communicative attitude, 140, 153; see also Kaiser, Hellmuth

Communicative relationship, from collaborative relationship to, 164–65

"Complementary reactions," 146n

Compulsive character: paranoid development from, 184–85; speech of, 63–65; urgency of problem presented by, 88–93; see also Obsessive character

Conflict: drive and defense formulations of neurotic, limitations of, 21–22; infantile neurotic, 18; internal, 43–50; internal, inhibitory reactions to anxiety of, 46–47; internal, self-estrangement and, 7, 8; therapist as subject of, 98–106

Conflict-generating organization of personality, 49

Conflict theory of psychoanalysis, classical, 14, 15–19; see also Psychoanalysis

Conscientiousness: driven and relentless, 30–32; obsessive, stages of therapeutic progress in cases of, 213–26; obsessive, urgency of presenting problem and, 90–93; obsessive indecision and, 38–40; see also Obsessive character

Consciousness: levels of, 11n; raising of, 118, 120, 121, 194; role in symptomatic behavior, 26–33; of role of patient, 160–63

Conservatism of personality, 200–201, 203; see also Resistance

Contact with the self and with therapist, 141–51; at termination of therapy, 233

235

Contemplative (observing) ego, 72–76

Contract, therapeutic, 79

Corrective reaction of restrictive attitudes, 194–96

Couch arrangement, 158–59; ease of talking and, 163–64

Course of therapy, 204–8; *see also* Change, therapeutic

Dangers of childhood, fantasied, 173–74

Decisions, self-imposed urgency to make, 90–93

Defense: against repressed infantile wish, interpretation of, 22; against unconscious homosexual wishes, paranoia as, 20–21, 181–85

Defense mechanisms as self-awareness–distorting reactions, 48–49

Denial, self-estrangement and, 13

Depression, stages of therapeutic progress in case of, 211–13

Developmental theory of libido, 17; Erikson's transformation of, 23

Development of neurosis, 177–78

Development of self-awareness in childhood, 137–39

Directed association technique, 18, 54

Disapproval of self, 5–6

Distortion of personality, 116

Distortion of self-awareness: by attitudes of personality, 32; defense mechanisms as reactions causing, 48–49; external observable evidence of, 40–41; instances of, 28–33; obsessive indecision and, 40; in reaction to termination of therapy, 232; restrictive attitudes and,

36–38; self-deceptive speech acts, 63–67, 142; self-estrangement and, 6–7; stages of articulation of levels of, 225

Domain of ego, enlargement of, 118, 122

Drinking problem, case of, 123–25; stages of therapeutic progress in, 208–11

Drive and defense formulation of neurotic conflict, limitations of, 21–22

Drive development, 23

Dynamics of subjective experience, *xi*, 36–50

Ego: concept of, 22; enlargement of domain of, 118, 122; observing, 72–76; theory of, 179; as therapeutic material, 56

Ego-alien symptom, 24

Ego and the Mechanisms of Defense, The (A. Freud), 55

Egocentric reactiveness, reversion to, 34–35

"Egocentric speech," 63*n*

"Ego deformity," characterological, 25–26

"Emotional" insight, 117

Empathy, 146*n*, 157; two pictures of patient and, 68

Erikson, Erik, 19, 23

Error of text analysis, 71–72

Estrangement from self, *see* Self-estrangement, neurotic

Expectations, patient's: presenting problem and, 78–82; of therapeutic relationship and therapist's attitude, 153–54; of therapist, 53

Index

External world, polarity between the self and, 33–36, 193; development of self-awareness in childhood and, 138–39; self-deceptive speech and, 66–67; therapeutic change and, 123–32

Fantasied dangers of childhood, 173–74
Fenichel, Otto, 12n, 71, 158n, 188n, 201n
Ferenczi, Sandor, 228
Free association, 18, 54, 71, 165
Freud, Anna, 55, 56, 202
Freud, Sigmund, 11n, 15–18, 20–21, 54, 73n, 96, 99, 101, 116n, 158–59, 160n, 165, 167, 169, 173–74, 176, 179n, 181, 183, 202, 206
Friedman, Lawrence, 73n

Gill, Merton M., 96n, 100n, 107n
Goals, therapeutic, 115–17; see also Change, therapeutic
Guided (directed) associations, 18, 54

"Here and now" recommendation, 61
Historical interpretation, 166–91; characterological understanding vs., 168–73; direct effect on patient, 185, 186–91; as intrinsically exculpatory, 188–89; of patient's reaction to termination of ther-

apy, 231–32; questions raised about, 166–68; source of anxiety and, 173–78; therapeutic handicaps of, 185–91; therapist and, 185–86; transference concept and, 179–85
Historical material, place in psychotherapy of, 189–91
Holt, Robert R., 23n
Homosexual wishes, paranoia as defense against unconscious, 20–21, 181–85
Hypnosis, 18, 54, 55, 165

Impressionability, example of, 44–45
Impulse, irresistible, 4
Indecision, obsessive, 38–40
Infant, subjective world of, 137–38
Infantile conflict, derivatives of, 18
Infantile experience, preserved, 170–73; understanding of neurotic anxiety in terms of, 173–74
Inhibitory reactions, continuously sustained, 46–47; see also Restrictive attitudes
Insight, 117–19
"Intellectual" insight, 117, 118
Intentionality, advances in, 121–23, 126
Internal change, changes in external relationships and stages of, 215
Internal conflict, 43–50; inhibitory reactions to anxiety of, 46–47; self-estrangement and, 7, 8
Interpretation, historical; see Historical interpretation
Involuntary response to communicative contact, 146–47, 149, 150
Irresistible impulse, 4

237

Index

101–2; perspective on problem, 83–86; reaction to termination of therapy, 231–33; relation to story, 94; termination of therapy by, 228; as therapeutic material, 57–61; two pictures of, 67–70, 76; see also Expectations, patient's; Problem, patient's; Transference

Personal history, therapeutic use of, see Historical interpretation

Piaget, Jean, 63n, 171

Polarity between the self and external world, 33–36, 193; development of self-awareness in childhood and, 138–39; self-deceptive speech and, 66–67; therapeutic change and, 123–32

Preconscious, 11, 11n

Presenting problem, 78–82

Problem, patient's, 77–94; presenting problem and patient's expectations, 78–82; of special urgency, 88–93; truth of patient's story, 93–94; two representations of same, 86–88; two views of, 83–86

Progress, nature of therapeutic, 208–26; in depression case, 211–13; in drinking problem case, 208–11; in obsessive cases, 213–26

Projection, defense mechanism of, 48

Psychoanalysis, basic rule of, 53, 54, 55, 63, 158, 159, 160, 202; classical conflict theory of, 14, 15–19; conception of neurosis in, 15–26; concept of the ego in, 22; defense mechanisms in, 48–49; division of mental processes in, 11, 11n; historical interpretation in, 166–73; Piaget's criticism of, 171; psychological structure in, 178; self-understanding and, 118–19; tradi-

tional relationship in, 157–65; trauma theory of neurosis in, 16–17; see also Analytic situation; Freud, Anna; Freud, Sigmund; Transference

Psychological structure, 178

Psychosexual development and conflict, 23

Psychotherapy: aim of, 10–13, 115–17; change in, 13, 115–39, 192–233; communicative attitude in, 140, 153; communicative contact in, 141–42, 149–51, 151n; "here and now" recommendation for, 61; historical interpretation in, 166–91; repetition in, 193–94; resistance in, 193–204; termination of, 226–33; see also Psychoanalysis; Therapeutic alliance; Therapeutic attitude; Therapeutic material; Therapeutic relationship

Purposefulness, articulation of subjective experience and, 119–23

Raising of consciousness, 118, 120, 121, 194

Rapaport, David, 11n

Reaction: "complementary," 146n; corrective, of restrictive attitudes, 194–96; involuntary, to communicative contact, 146–47, 149, 150; to the self, therapeutic change and, 133–37; to termination of therapy, 231–33

Reactions to therapist, 95–111; expression of therapeutic relationship and, 106–11; as subject of conflict, 98–106

Index

continuous, 43; patient's picture of himself as, 69, 70; question of "observing ego" and, 72–76; termination of therapy and, 229; therapist's failure to recognize patient's, 148

Self-deceptive speech acts, 63–67, 142

Self-estrangement, neurotic, 3–10; characterological interpretation of, 172–73; denial and, 13; diminished, recognition of objective reality and, 36; distortion of self-awareness and, 6–7; instances of, 4 8, 28 33; internal conflict and, 7, 8; nuclear-conflict theory and, 24–25; in symptomatic behavior and reaction, 27–33

Self-psychology, 23, 25–26

Self-regulating capacities, 42–43, 201

Self-understanding, therapeutic change through, 117–19

Separation and loss, reaction to termination as, 231

Sexual seduction theory, 16, 17

Shapiro, David, 15n, 19n, 48n, 64n, 123n, 138n

Shaw, George Bernard, 154 56

"Sign-situations," 67n

Speaker, relation of, to words used, 62–67

Speech: aims of, 63; "egocentric," 63n; of obsessive-compulsive individuals, 63–65; present reason for patient's, 61; self-conscious form of, 161

Speech acts, 62–67, 97–98; error of text analysis of, 71–72; expression of therapeutic relationship and, 106–11; how something is said,

62; self-deceptive, 63–67, 142; of therapist, 110; two pictures of patient from, 67–70

Spence, Donald, 167–68

Stern, Daniel N., 137n

Structure, psychological, 178

Subjective dynamics of neurotic conflict, therapeutic progress in unfolding of, 218–26

Subjective experience: dynamics of, xi, 36–50; historical interpretation as distraction from present, 186–91; quality of unarticulated, 129–30; see also Articulation of subjective experience

Subjective world: characteristic, 27; of infant, 137–38

Symptom, neurotic: change in psychiatric picture of, 24; changes of obsessive, during therapeutic progress, 213–14, 225–26; as characterological, 26–27; as medical-psychological problem, 19; as product of dynamics of personality, 37; in trauma theory, 16

Symptom analysis, 169

Symptomatic behavior: consciousness and, 26–33; restrictive attitudes and, 36 37; subjective estrangement from, 27–33

Symptomatic improvement, terminating therapy and, 228

Symptom neurosis, 15, 25

Tähkä, Veikko, 146n

Tension: articulation of, 119–23; restrictive personality and continuous state of, 43–50; see also Conflict